Congratulations!

s a student purchasing *Designing the User Interface: Fourth Edition Preview*, you are entitled to x months of prepaid access to the book's Companion Web site. This site contains additional pre-ew material not available in the printed fourth edition preview text.

) access the *Designing the User Interface: Fourth Edition Preview* Companion Web site or the first time:

1) Go to **http://www.aw.com/shneiderman**.
2) Click **Fourth Edition Preview Materials**.
3) Click the **Register** button.
4) Use a coin to scratch off the gray coating below and reveal your student access code.* Do not use a knife or other sharp object, which can damage the code.

D1136881

5) On the registration page, enter your student access code. Do not type the dashes. You can use lowercase or uppercase letters.
6) Follow the on-screen instructions. If you need help at any time during the online registration process, simply click the **Need Help?** icon.
7) Once your personal Login Name and Password are confirmed, you can begin using the *Designing the User Interface: Fourth Edition Preview* Companion Web site!

)u will need to register online using a computer with an Internet connection and a Web browser. ıe process takes just a couple of minutes and only needs to be completed once.

) log into the *Designing the User Interface: Fourth Edition Preview* Companion Web te after you register:

)u only need to register for this Companion Web site once. After that, you can access the site by)ing to http://www.aw.com/shneiderman, clicking "Fourth Edition Preview Materials," and provid-g your Login Name and Password when prompted.

mportant: The Access Code on this page can only be used once to establish a subscription to the *esigning the User Interface: Fourth Edition Preview* Companion Web site. This subscription is valid r six months upon activation and is not transferable. If this access code has already been scratched f, it may no longer be valid. If this is the case, you can purchase a subscription by going to tp://www.aw.com/shneiderman and clicking "Fourth Edition Preview Materials."

Designing the User Interface

Strategies for Effective Human-Computer Interaction

Fourth Edition Preview

Ben Shneiderman
Catherine Plaisant
University of Maryland

Boston San Francisco New York
London Toronto Sydney Tokyo Singapore Madrid
Mexico City Munich Paris Cape Town Hong Kong Montreal

Senior Acquisitions Editor	Maite Suarez-Rivas
Editorial Assistant	Maria Campo
Senior Marketing Coordinator	Lesly Hershman
Senior Production Supervisor	Jeffrey Holcomb
Project Management	Argosy Publishing
Copyeditor	Rachel Wheeler
Proofreader	Kim Cofer
Composition and Art	Argosy Publishing
Text Designer	Joyce Cosentino Wells
Text Image	© 2003 Photodisc, Getty Images
Cover Image	© 2003 Boris Lyubner, SIS
Prepress and Manufacturing	Caroline Fell

Access the latest information about Addison-Wesley titles from our World Wide Web site:
http://www.aw.com/cs

ISBN 0-321-19785-2
1 2 3 4 5 6 7 8 9 10-CRS-06 05 04 03

Contents

Essay 2

Essay 3

Essay 4

chapter

Human Factors of Interactive Software

Designing an object to be simple and clear takes at least twice as long as the usual way. It requires concentration at the outset on how a clear and simple system would work, followed by the steps required to make it come out that way—steps which are often much harder and more complex than the ordinary ones. It also requires relentless pursuit of that simplicity even when obstacles appear which would seem to stand in the way of that simplicity.

T. H. NELSON

The Home Computer Revolution, 1977

Page Proofs
Non-Finalized Files

1.1 Introduction

New technologies provide extraordinary—almost supernatural—powers to those people who master them. Networked computer systems and advanced interfaces are compelling new technologies that are being rapidly disseminated. Great excitement spreads as designers provide remarkable functions in carefully crafted interactive devices and systems. The opportunities for youthful designers and mature entrepreneurs are substantial, and the impacts on individuals, organizations, and cultures are profound.

Like early photography equipment or automobiles, early computers were usable only by people who devoted effort to mastering the technology. Harnessing the computer's power is a task for designers who combine an understanding of technology with a sensitivity to human capacities and needs.

Human performance and user experience with computer and information systems will remain a rapidly expanding research and development topic in the coming decades. This interdisciplinary design science began by combining the data-gathering methods and intellectual framework of experimental psychology with the powerful and widely used tools developed from computer science. Then contributions accrued from educational and industrial psychologists, instructional and graphic designers, technical writers, experts in human factors or ergonomics, information systems specialists, and adventuresome anthropologists and sociologists. And now, as computers and user interfaces are becoming the basis for increasingly powerful sociotechnical systems, policy analysts, economists, lawyers, privacy advocates, and ethicists are playing a growing role.

User interfaces help produce business news stories and Wall Street sensations such as America Online and eBay. They also produce intense competition (with Microsoft as a favorite enemy), copyright-infringement suits, intellectual property battles, mega-mergers, and international partnerships. User interfaces are often controversial because of their central role in national identification schemes, homeland defense, crime fighting, medical records management, etc. In the aftermath of the September 11, 2001 terror attacks, members of Congress discussed the inadequacies of FBI user interfaces to support searches for terrorists.

At an individual level, user interfaces change many people's lives: effective user interfaces mean that doctors can make more accurate diagnoses, children can learn more effectively, graphic artists can explore creative possibilities more fluidly, and pilots can fly airplanes more safely. Some changes, however, are disruptive; too often, users must cope with frustration, fear, and failure when they encounter excessive complexity, incomprehensible terminology, or chaotic layouts.

The steadily growing interest in user-interface design spans remarkably diverse systems (Figs. 1.1 to 1.7 and Color Plates A1 to A6). Word processors and desktop-publishing tools are used routinely, while digital photos and voice messaging have become familiar. Electronic mail, instant messaging, and videoconferencing provide new personal and business communication media. A remarkable number of people take advantage of the World Wide Web's remarkable educational resources, government services, and online communities. Technical users benefit from image and data libraries in applications from medicine to space exploration. Scientific visualization and simulator workstations allow safe experimentation and inexpensive training. Analysts from many disciplines have come to depend on electronic spreadsheets and decision-support systems. Commercial systems include inventory, personnel, reservations, air-traffic, and electric-utility control. Software-engineering environments allow rapid prototyping, as do computer-assisted design, manufacturing, and engineering workstations. Many people use consumer electronics, such as DVDs, cameras, cell phones, and portable information appliances. Art, music, sports, and entertainment all are available by way of convenient user interfaces.

Figure 1.1

Macintosh System 9.2. The active window, which shows stripes in the title bar, is on top. Windows can be dragged partially off the display to the left, right, and bottom. File and folder icons can be dragged to new folders or to the trash can for deletion.

Making these diverse applications successful requires contributions from researchers and practitioners in many fields. Academic and industrial researchers are developing descriptive taxonomies, explanatory theories, predictive models, and prescriptive guidance, while experimenters are collecting empirical data as a basis for new theories. The motor, perceptual, and cognitive foundations are growing firmer, while the social, economic, and ethical impacts are becoming clearer.

Information architects are exploring how best to organize knowledge resources and graphic designers are inventing alternative presentations. Software designers are developing query languages and visual strategies for input, search, and output. They are using sound (such as music and voice), three-dimensional representations, animation, and video to improve the appeal and information content of interfaces. Techniques such as direct manipulation, telepresence, and virtual realities may change the ways that we interact with and think about technology and our work.

Hardware developers and system builders are offering novel input and pointing devices, as well as large, high-resolution color displays. They are

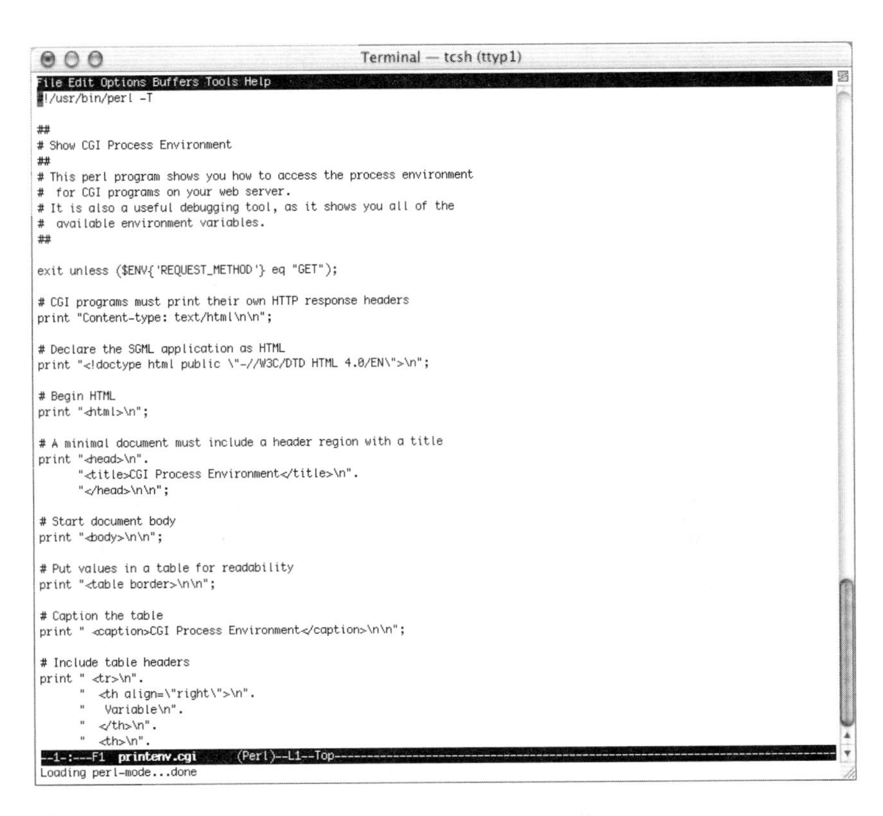

Figure 1.2

Macintosh System 10.2 has a Unix commmand line terminal integrated into the traditional Macintosh windows-based operating system.

designing systems that both provide rapid response times for increasingly complex tasks and have fast display rates and smooth transitions for increasingly complex three-dimensional manipulations. Technologies that allow speech input and output, gestural input, and tactile or force-feedback output increase ease of use, as do input devices such as the touchscreen and three-dimensional scanners.

Developers with an orientation toward educational psychology, instructional design, and technical writing are creating engaging online tutorials, training materials, reference manuals, demonstrations, and sales materials. They are exploring novel approaches to group lectures, distance learning, and collaborative experiences. Graphic designers are actively engaged in visual layout, color selection, and animation. Sociologists, anthropologists, philosophers, policymakers, and managers are dealing with organizational impact, computer anxiety, job redesign, retraining, distributed teamwork,

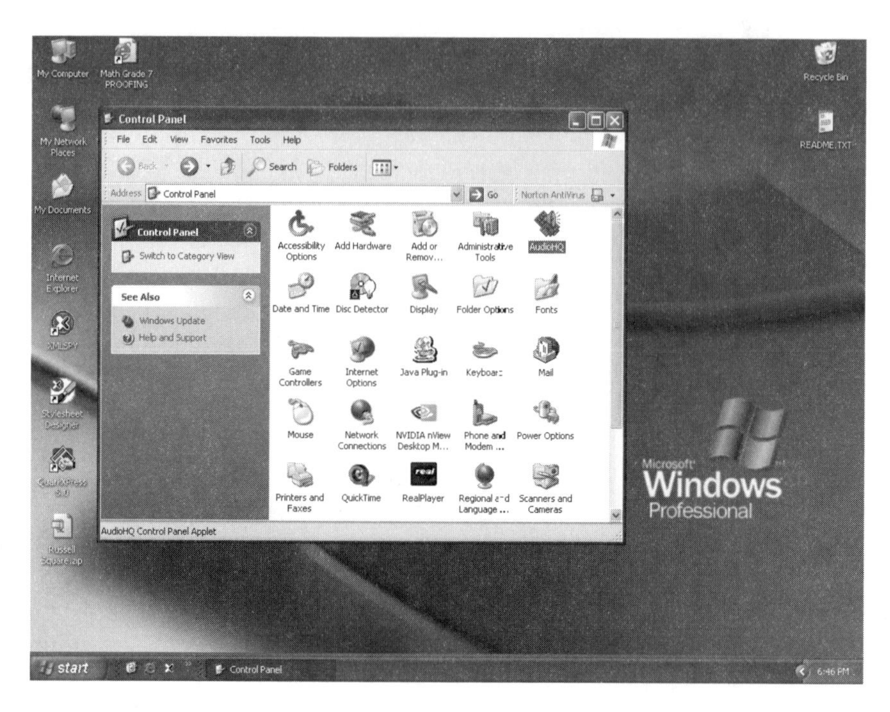

Figure 1.3

A Microsoft Windows XP desktop with its control panel open.

computer-supported cooperation strategies, work-at-home schemes, and long-term societal changes.

Product designers face the challenge of providing services on small portable devices such as cell phones or pocket computers, standard desktop PCs or laptops, public kiosks, and large-sized plasma panels or projected displays. The plasticity of their designs must ensure smooth conversion to speech, delivery by way of Web browsers, translation into multiple languages, and compatibility with accessibility-support devices for handicapped users.

We are living in an exciting time for developers of user interfaces. The hardware and software foundations for the bridges and tunnels have been built. Now the roadway can be laid and the stripes painted to make way for the heavy traffic of eager users.

The rapid growth of interest in user-interface design is international in scope. In the United States, the Association for Computing Machinery (ACM) Special Interest Group in Computer Human Interaction (SIGCHI) had more than 6000 members in 2003. The annual CHI conferences can

Figure 1.4

The LeapFrog LeapPad is among the most popular interactive toys for children. It gives voice instructions and feedback during reading drills and games.

draw 3000 people. The Usability Professionals Association focuses on commercial approaches, and the Human Factors & Ergonomics Society, the American Society for Information Science & Technology, and other professional groups attend to research on human-computer interaction. Graphic designers participate in the American Institute for Graphic Artists (AIGA), and technical writers interested in user interfaces are active in the Society for Technical Communications (STC). Interface-design issues are also increasingly common topics at conferences for software engineers, biologists, geographers, law enforcers, financial analysts, and military technologists. Regular conferences in Europe, Japan, and elsewhere draw substantial audiences of researchers and practitioners. The European Commission's 6th Framework Programme will devote 3.6 billion euros to information technology research during 2002–2006. In Japan, the Ministry of International Trade and Industry promotes commercially oriented projects and consortia among many companies.

This chapter gives a broad overview of human-computer interaction from practitioner and research perspectives. Specific references cited in the chapter appear on page 37, and a set of general references begins on page 38.

1.2 Goals of System Engineering

Every designer wants to build a high-quality interactive system that is admired by colleagues, celebrated by users, circulated widely, and imitated frequently. Appreciation comes not from flamboyant promises or stylish advertising, but rather from inherent quality features that are achieved through thoughtful planning, sensitivity to user needs, and diligent testing.

Managers can promote attention to user-interface design by selection of personnel, preparation of schedules and milestones, construction and application of guidelines documents, and commitment to testing. Designers then propose multiple design alternatives for consideration, and the leading contenders are subjected to further development and testing (see Chapters 3 and 4). User-interface–building tools (see Chapter 5) enable rapid implementation and easy revision. Evaluation of designs refines the understanding of appropriateness for each choice.

Successful designers go beyond the vague notion of "user friendliness," probing deeper than simply making a checklist of subjective guidelines. They have a thorough understanding of the diverse community of users and the tasks that must be accomplished. Moreover, they are deeply committed to serving the users, which strengthens their resolve when they face the pressures of short deadlines, tight budgets, and weak-willed compromisers.

Effective systems generate positive feelings of success, competence, mastery, and clarity in the user community. The users are not encumbered by the computer and can predict what will happen in response to each of their actions. When an interactive system is well designed, the interface almost disappears, enabling users to concentrate on their work, exploration, or pleasure. Creating an environment in which tasks are carried out almost effortlessly and users are "in the flow" requires a great deal of hard work by the designer.

Setting explicit goals helps designers to achieve those goals. In getting beyond the vague quest for user-friendly systems, managers and designers can focus on specific goals that include well-defined system engineering and measurable human-factors objectives. The U.S. Military Standard for Human Engineering Design Criteria (1999) states these purposes:

- Achieve required performance by operator, control, and maintenance personnel
- Minimize skill and personnel requirements and training time

- Achieve required reliability of personnel-equipment/software combinations
- Foster design standardization within and among systems

Effective systems should also enhance the quality of life for users. Setting such goals is controversial and varies across cultures—these broader issues are left for the Afterword.

1.2.1 Proper functionality

The first step is to ascertain the necessary functionality—i.e., what tasks and subtasks must be carried out. The frequent tasks are easy to determine, but the occasional tasks, the exceptional tasks for emergency conditions, and the repair tasks to cope with errors in use of the system are more difficult to discover. Task analysis is central, because systems with inadequate functionality frustrate the user and are often rejected or underutilized. If the functionality is inadequate, it does not matter how well the user interface is designed. Providing excessive functionality (which is probably the more common mistake of designers) is also a danger, because the clutter and complexity make implementation, maintenance, learning, and usage more difficult.

1.2.2 Reliability, availability, security, and data integrity

A vital second step is ensuring proper system reliability: commands must function as specified, displayed data must reflect the database contents, and updates must be applied correctly. Users' trust of systems is fragile; one experience with misleading data or unexpected results will undermine for a long time a person's willingness to use a system. The software architecture, hardware components, and network support must ensure high availability. If the system is not available or introduces errors, it does not matter how well the human interface is designed. Designers also must pay attention to ensuring privacy, security, and data integrity. Protection must be provided from unauthorized access, inadvertent destruction of data, and malicious tampering.

1.2.3 Standardization, integration, consistency, and portability

As the number of users and software packages increases, the pressures for and benefits of standardization grow. Slight differences between systems not only increase learning times but also can lead to annoying and dangerous errors. Gross differences between systems require substantial retraining and burden users in many ways. Incompatible storage formats, hardware, and software versions cause frustration, inefficiency, and delay. Designers must decide whether the improvements they offer are useful enough to offset the disruption to the users.

Standardization refers to common user-interface features across multiple applications. Apple Computers (1992, 2002) successfully developed an early standard that was widely applied by thousands of developers, enabling users to learn multiple applications quickly. When the Microsoft Windows (1999, 2001) interface became standardized, it became a powerful force.

Integration across application packages and software tools was one of the key design principles in Unix. (Portability across hardware platforms was another.) If file formats are used consistently, users can apply multiple applications to transform, refine, or validate their data.

Consistency primarily refers to common action sequences, terms, units, layouts, color, typography, and so on within an application program. Consistency is a strong determinant of success of systems. It is naturally extended to include compatibility across application programs and compatibility with paper or non–computer-based systems. Compatibility across versions is a troubling demand, since the desire to accommodate novel functionality or improved designs competes with the benefits of consistency.

Portability refers to the potential to convert data and to share user interfaces across multiple software and hardware environments. Arranging for portability is a challenge for designers, who must contend with different display sizes and resolutions, color capabilities, pointing devices, data formats, and so on. Some user-interface–building tools help by generating code for Macintosh, Windows, Unix, and other environments, so that the interfaces are similar in each environment or resemble the style in those environments. Standard text files (in ASCII) can be moved easily across environments, but graphic images, spreadsheets, video images, and so on are more difficult to convert.

1.2.4 Schedules and budgets

Careful planning and courageous management are needed if a project is to be completed on schedule and within budget. Delayed delivery or cost overruns can threaten a system because of the confrontational political atmosphere in a company, or because the competitive market environment contains potentially overwhelming forces. If an in-house system is delivered late, other projects may be affected, and the disruption may cause managers to choose to install an alternative system. If a commercial system is too costly, customer resistance may emerge to prevent widespread acceptance, allowing competitors to capture the market.

Proper attention to human-factors principles and rigorous testing often lead to reduced cost and rapid development. A carefully tested design generates fewer changes during implementation and avoids costly updates after release. The business case for human factors in computer and information systems is strong (Landauer, 1995; Norman, 2000), as demonstrated by many successful products whose advantage lay in their superior user interfaces.

1.3 Goals of User-Interface Design

If adequate functionality has been chosen, reliability is ensured, standardization has been addressed, and scheduling and budgetary planning are complete, developers can focus their attention on the design and testing process. Multiple design alternatives must be evaluated for specific user communities and for specific benchmark tasks. A clever design for one community of users may be inappropriate for another community. An efficient design for one class of tasks may be inefficient for another class.

The relativity of design played a central role in the evolution of information services at the Library of Congress (Marchionini *et al.*, 1993). Two of the major uses of computer systems were cataloging new books and searching the online book catalog. Separate systems for these tasks were created that optimized the design for one task but made the complementary task difficult. It was impossible to say which was better, because both were fine systems, but they were serving different needs—posing such a question would be like asking whether the New York Philharmonic Orchestra was better than the New York Yankees baseball team.

The situation became even more complex when Congressional staffers and then the public were invited to use the search systems. Three- to six-hour training courses were appropriate for Congressional staffers, but the first-time public users were overwhelmed by the command language and complex cataloging rules. Eventually a touchscreen interface with reduced functionality and better information presentation was developed and became a big success in the public reading rooms. The next step in evolution was the development of a World Wide Web version of the catalog to allow users anywhere in the world to access the catalog and other databases. These changing user communities and requirements each led to interface changes, even though the database and services remained similar.

Careful determination of the user community and of the benchmark set of tasks is the basis for establishing human-factors goals. For each user and each task, precise measurable objectives guide the designer, evaluator, purchaser, or manager. These five measurable human factors are central to evaluation:

1. *Time to learn.* How long does it take for typical members of the user community to learn how to use the commands relevant to a set of tasks?
2. *Speed of performance.* How long does it take to carry out the benchmark tasks?
3. *Rate of errors by users.* How many and what kinds of errors do people make in carrying out the benchmark tasks? Although time to make and correct errors might be incorporated into the speed of performance, error handling is such a critical component of system usage that it deserves extensive study.
4. *Retention over time.* How well do users maintain their knowledge after an hour, a day, or a week? Retention may be linked closely to time to learn, and frequency of use plays an important role.
5. *Subjective satisfaction.* How much did users like using various aspects of the system? The answer can be ascertained by interview or by written surveys that include satisfaction scales and space for free-form comments.

Every designer would like to succeed in every category, but there are often forced tradeoffs. If lengthy learning is permitted, task-performance times may be reduced by use of complex abbreviations, macros, and shortcuts. If the rate of errors is to be kept extremely low, speed of performance may have to be sacrificed. In some applications, subjective satisfaction may be the key determinant of success; in others, short learning times or rapid performance may be paramount. Project managers and designers must be aware of the tradeoffs and must make their choices explicit and public. Requirements documents and marketing brochures should make clear which goals are primary.

After multiple design alternatives have been raised, the leading possibilities should be reviewed by designers and users. Low-fidelity paper mockups are useful, but high-fidelity online prototypes create a more realistic environment for review. First, design teams should negotiate the guidelines document to make explicit the permissible formats, sequences, terminology, and so on. Once the interface design has been created with suitable prototyping tools, testing can begin to ensure that the user-interface design goals have been met. The user manual and the technical reference manual can be written before the implementation to provide another review and perspective on the design. Next, the implementation can be carried out with proper software tools; this task should be a modest one if the design is complete and precise. Finally, the acceptance test certifies that the delivered system meets the goals of the designers and customers. The development and evaluation process is described in greater detail in Chapters 3 and 4.

1.4 Motivations for Human Factors in Design

The enormous interest in human factors of interactive systems arises from the complementary recognition of how poorly designed many current systems are and how genuinely developers desire to create elegant systems that serve the users effectively. This increased concern emanates from four primary sources: life-critical systems; industrial and commercial uses; office, home, and entertainment applications; and exploratory, creative, and cooperative systems.

1.4.1 Life-critical systems

Life-critical systems include those that control air traffic, nuclear reactors, power utilities, staffed spacecraft, police or fire dispatch, military operations, and medical instruments. In these applications high costs are expected, but they should yield high reliability and effectiveness. Lengthy training periods are acceptable to obtain rapid, error-free performance, even when the users are under stress. Subjective satisfaction is less of an issue because the users are well motivated. Retention is obtained by frequent use of common functions and practice sessions for emergency actions.

1.4.2 Industrial and commercial uses

Typical industrial and commercial uses include banking, insurance, order entry, inventory management, airline and hotel reservations, car rentals, utility billing, credit-card management, and point-of-sales terminals. In these cases, costs shape many judgments; lower cost may be preferred even if there is some sacrifice in reliability. Operator training time is expensive, so ease of learning is important. The tradeoffs for speed of performance and error rates are governed by the total cost over the system's lifetime. Subjective satisfaction is of modest importance; retention is obtained by frequent use. Speed of performance becomes central for most of these applications because of the high volume of transactions, but operator fatigue or burnout is a legitimate concern. Trimming 10% off the mean transaction time means 10% fewer operators, 10% fewer terminal workstations, and possibly a 10% reduction in hardware costs.

1.4.3 Office, home, and entertainment applications

The rapid expansion of office, home, and entertainment applications is the third source of interest in human factors. Personal-computing applications include word processing, automated transaction machines, video games, educational packages, information retrieval, electronic mail, computer conferencing, and small-business management. For these systems, ease of learning, low error rates, and subjective satisfaction are paramount because use is frequently discretionary and competition is fierce. If the users cannot succeed quickly, they will abandon the use of a computer or try a competing package. In cases where use is intermittent, retention is likely to be faulty, so online assistance becomes important.

Choosing the right functionality is difficult. Novices are best served by a constrained, simple set of actions, but as users' experience increases, so does their desire for more extensive functionality and rapid performance. A layered or level-structured design is one approach to graceful evolution from novice to expert usage. Low cost is important because of lively competition, but extensive design and testing expenses can be amortized over the large number of users.

1.4.4 Exploratory, creative, and cooperative systems

An increasing fraction of computer use is dedicated to supporting human intellectual and creative enterprises. Electronic encyclopedias, World Wide Web browsing, collaborative writing, statistical hypothesis formation, business decision making, and graphical presentation of scientific simulation results are examples of exploratory environments. Creative environments include writer's toolkits or workbenches, architecture or automobile design systems, artist or programmer workstations, and music-composition systems. Decision-support tools aid knowledgeable users in medical diagnosis, finance, industrial-process management, and military command and control. Cooperative systems enable two or more people to work together, even if the users are separated by time and space, through use of electronic text, voice, and video mail; through electronic meeting systems that facilitate face-to-face meetings; or through groupware that enables remote collaborators to work concurrently on a document, map, spreadsheet, or image.

In these systems, the users may be knowledgeable in the task domain but novices in the underlying computer concepts. Their motivation is often high, but so are their expectations. Benchmark tasks are more difficult to describe because of the exploratory nature of these applications. Usage can range from occasional to frequent. In short, it is difficult to design and evaluate these systems. At best, designers can pursue the goal of having the computer vanish as users become completely absorbed in their task domains. This goal seems to be met most effectively when the computer provides a direct-manipulation representation of the world of action. Then, tasks are carried out by rapid familiar selections or gestures, with immediate feedback and new sets of choices.

1.5 Universal Usability

The remarkable diversity of human abilities, backgrounds, motivations, personalities, and work styles challenges interactive-system designers. A right-handed female designer with computer training and a desire for rapid interaction using densely packed screens may have a hard time developing a successful workstation for left-handed male artists with a more leisurely and free-form work style. Understanding the physical, intellectual, and personality differences between users is vital for expanding market share, supporting required government services, and enabling creative participation by the broadest possible set of users. As a profession, we will be remembered for how well we address the needs of all users.

1.5.1 Physical abilities and physical workplaces

Accommodating diverse human perceptual, cognitive, and motor abilities is a challenge to every designer. Fortunately, there is much literature reporting research and experience from design projects with automobiles, aircraft, typewriters, home appliances, and so on that can be applied to the design of interactive computer systems. In a sense, the presence of a computer is only incidental to the design; human needs and abilities are the guiding forces.

Basic data about human dimensions comes from research in *anthropometry* (Dreyfuss, 1967; Pheasant, 1996). Thousands of measures of hundreds of features of people—male and female, young and adult, European and Asian, underweight and overweight, and tall and short—provide data to construct means and 5- to 95-percentile groupings. Head, mouth, nose, neck, shoulder, chest, arm, hand, finger, leg, and foot sizes have been carefully cataloged for a variety of populations. The great diversity in these static measures reminds us that there can be no image of an "average" user, and that compromises must be made or multiple versions of a system must be constructed.

The choice of keyboard design parameters—in terms of distance between keys, size of keys, and required pressure (see Section 9.2)—evolved to accommodate the differences between the physical abilities of users. People with especially large or small hands may have difficulty in using standard keyboards, but a substantial fraction of the population is well served by one design. On the other hand, since screen-brightness preferences vary substantially, designers must provide a knob to enable user control. Controls for chair seat and back heights and for display-screen angles also allow individual adjustment. When a single design cannot accommodate a large fraction of the population, multiple versions or adjustment controls are helpful.

Physical measures of static human dimensions are not enough. Measures of dynamic actions—such as reach distance while seated, speed of finger presses, or strength of lifting—are also necessary (Bailey, 1996).

Since so much of work is related to perception, designers need to be aware of the ranges of human perceptual abilities (Ware, 2000). Vision is especially important and has been thoroughly studied (Wickens and Hollands, 2000). For example, researchers consider human response time to varying visual stimuli, or time to adapt to low or bright light. They examine human capacity to identify an object in context, or to determine the velocity or direction of a moving point. The visual system responds differently to various colors, and some people are colorblind. People's spectral range and sensitivity vary, and peripheral vision is quite different from perception of images in the fovea. Flicker, contrast, and motion sensitivity must be considered, as must the impact of glare and of visual fatigue. Depth perception, which allows three-dimensional viewing, is based on several cues. Some viewing angles and distances make the screen easier to read. Finally, designers must consider the needs of people who have eye disorders, damage, or disease, or who wear corrective lenses.

Other senses are also important: for example, touch for keyboard or touchscreen entry, and hearing for audible cues, tones, and speech input or output (see Chapter 9). Pain, temperature sensitivity, taste, and smell are rarely used for input or output in interactive systems, but there is room for imaginative applications.

These physical abilities influence elements of the interactive-system design. They also play a prominent role in the design of the workplace or workstation (or playstation). The draft standard *Human Factors Engineering of Computer Workstations* (2002) lists these concerns:

- Work-surface and display-support height
- Clearance under work surface for legs
- Work-surface width and depth
- Adjustability of heights and angles for chairs and work surfaces
- Posture—seating depth and angle; back-rest height and lumbar support
- Availability of armrests, footrests, and palmrests
- Use of chair casters

Workplace design is important in ensuring high job satisfaction, high performance, and low error rates. Incorrect table heights, uncomfortable chairs, or inadequate space to place documents can substantially impede work. The standard document also addresses such issues as illumination levels (200 to 500 lux); glare reduction (antiglare coatings, baffles, mesh, positioning); luminance balance and flicker; equipment reflectivity; acoustic noise and vibration; air temperature, movement, and humidity; and equipment temperature.

The most elegant screen design can be compromised by a noisy environment, poor lighting, or a stuffy room, and that compromise will eventually lower performance, raise error rates, and discourage even motivated users.

Another physical-environment consideration involves room layout and the sociology of human interaction. With multiple workstations for a classroom or office, alternate layouts can encourage or limit social interaction, cooperative work, and assistance with problems. Because users can often quickly help one another with minor problems, there may be an advantage to layouts that group several terminals close together or that enable supervisors or teachers to view all screens at once from behind. On the other hand, programmers, reservations clerks, or artists may appreciate the quiet and privacy of their own workspace.

The physical design of workplaces is often discussed under the term *ergonomics*. Anthropometry, sociology, industrial psychology, organizational behavior studies, and anthropology may offer useful insights in this area.

1.5.2 Cognitive and perceptual abilities

A vital foundation for interactive-systems designers is an understanding of the cognitive and perceptual abilities of the users (Wickens and Hollands, 2000; Ashcraft, 2001; Goldstein, 2002). The human ability to interpret sensory input rapidly and to initiate complex actions makes modern computer systems possible. In milliseconds, users recognize slight changes on their displays and begin to issue streams of commands. The journal *Ergonomics Abstracts* offers this classification of human cognitive processes:

- Short-term memory
- Long-term memory and learning
- Problem solving
- Decision making
- Attention and set (scope of concern)
- Search and scanning
- Time perception

They also suggest this set of factors affecting perceptual and motor performance:

- Arousal and vigilance
- Fatigue
- Perceptual (mental) load
- Knowledge of results
- Monotony and boredom
- Sensory deprivation
- Sleep deprivation
- Anxiety and fear
- Isolation
- Aging
- Drugs and alcohol
- Circadian rhythms

These vital issues are not discussed in depth in this book, but they have a profound influence on the quality of the design of most interactive systems. The term *intelligence* is not included in this list, because its nature is controversial and measuring pure intelligence is difficult.

In any application, background experience and knowledge in the task domain and the interface domain (see Section 2.3) play key roles in learning and performance. Task- or computer-skill inventories can be helpful in predicting performance.

1.5.3 Personality differences

Some people dislike computers or are made anxious by them; others are attracted to or are eager to use computers. Often, members of these divergent groups disapprove or are suspicious of members of the other community. Even people who enjoy using computers may have very different preferences for interaction styles, pace of interaction, graphics versus tabular presentations, dense versus sparse data presentation, step-by-step work versus all-at-once work, and so on. These differences are important. A clear understanding of personality and cognitive styles can be helpful in designing systems for a specific community of users.

A fundamental difference is one between men and women, but no clear pattern of preferences has been documented. It is often pointed out that the preponderance of video-arcade game players and designers are young males. There are women players of any game, but popular choices among women for early video games were Pacman and its variants, plus a few other games such as Donkey Kong and Tetris. We have only speculations regarding why women prefer these games. One female commentator labeled Pacman "oral aggressive" and could appreciate the female style of play. Other women have identified the compulsive cleaning up of every dot as an attraction. These games are distinguished by their less violent action and soundtracks. Also, the board is fully visible, characters have personality, softer color patterns are used, and there is a sense of closure and completeness. Can these informal conjectures be converted to measurable criteria and then validated? While early game designers focused on the needs and desires of men and boys, many newer games are more attractive to women. For example, The Sims and its online version are innovative simulations of families that attract more female purchasers and players than males.

Turning from games to office automation, the largely male designers may not realize the effects on women users when command names require the users to KILL a file or ABORT a program. These and other potential unfortunate mismatches between the user interface and the user might be avoided by more thoughtful attention to individual differences among users. Huff (1987) found a bias when he asked teachers to design educational games for boys or girls. The designers created gamelike challenges when they expected boys as users and used more conversational dialogs when they expected girls as users. When told to design for students, the designers produced boy-style games.

Unfortunately, there is no simple taxonomy of user personality types. A popular technique is to use the Myers-Briggs Type Indicator (MBTI) (Keirsey, 1998), which is based on Carl Jung's theories of personality types. Jung conjectured that there were four dichotomies:

- *Extroversion versus introversion.* Extroverts focus on external stimuli and like variety and action, whereas introverts prefer familiar patterns, rely on their inner ideas, and work alone contentedly.
- *Sensing versus intuition.* Sensing types are attracted to established routines, are good at precise work, and enjoy applying known skills, whereas intuitive types like solving new problems and discovering new relations but dislike taking time for precision.
- *Perceptive versus judging.* Perceptive types like to learn about new situations but may have trouble making decisions, whereas judging types like to make a careful plan and will seek to carry through the plan even if new facts change the goal.
- *Feeling versus thinking.* Feeling types are aware of other people's feelings, seek to please others, and relate well to most people, whereas thinking types are unemotional, may treat people impersonally, and like to put things in logical order.

The theory behind the MBTI provides portraits of the relationships between professions and personality types and between people of different personality types. It has been applied to testing of user communities and has provided guidance for designers.

Many hundreds of psychological scales have been developed, including risk taking versus risk avoidance; internal versus external locus of control; reflective versus impulsive behavior; convergent versus divergent thinking; high versus low anxiety; tolerance for stress; tolerance for ambiguity, motivation, or compulsiveness; field dependence versus independence; assertive versus passive personality; and left- versus right-brain orientation. As designers explore computer applications for home, education, art, music, and entertainment, they will benefit from paying greater attention to personality types.

1.5.4 Cultural and international diversity

Another perspective on individual differences has to do with cultural, ethnic, racial, or linguistic background (Fernandes, 1995; Marcus and

Gould, 2000). It seems obvious that users who were raised learning to read Japanese or Chinese will scan a screen differently from users who were raised learning to read English or French. Users from cultures that have a more reflective style or respect for ancestral traditions may prefer interfaces different from those chosen by users from cultures that are more action-oriented or novelty-based.

More and more is being learned about computer users from different cultures, but designers are still struggling to establish guidelines for designing for multiple languages and cultures. The growth of a worldwide computer market (many U.S. companies have more than half of their sales in overseas markets) means that designers must prepare for internationalization. Software architectures that facilitate customization of local versions of user interfaces should be emphasized. For example, all text (instructions, help, error messages, labels, etc.) might be stored in files, so that versions in other languages can be generated with no or little additional programming. Hardware concerns include character sets, keyboards, and special input devices. User-interface design concerns for internationalization include the following:

- Characters, numerals, special characters, and diacriticals
- Left-to-right versus right-to-left versus vertical input and reading
- Date and time formats
- Numeric and currency formats
- Weights and measures
- Telephone numbers and addresses
- Names and titles (Mr., Ms., Mme., M., Dr.)
- Social security, national identification, and passport numbers
- Capitalization and punctuation
- Sorting sequences
- Icons, buttons, and colors
- Pluralization, grammar, and spelling
- Etiquette, policies, tone, formality, and metaphors

The list is long and yet incomplete. Whereas early designers were often excused from cultural and linguistic slips, the current highly competitive atmosphere means that more effective localization will often produce a strong advantage. To promote effective designs, companies should run usability studies with users from different countries, cultures, and language communities.

1.5.5 Users with disabilities

The flexibility of desktop and Web software makes it possible for designers to provide special services to users who have disabilities (Edwards, 1995; Vanderheiden, 2000; Paciello, 2000; Stephanidis, 2001). In the U.S., the 1998 Amendment to Section 508 of the Rehabilitation Act requires Federal agencies to ensure access to information technology, including computers and Web sites, by employees and the public. The Access Board spells out the implications for vision-impaired, hearing-impaired, and mobility-impaired users, such as keyboard or mouse alternatives, color coding, font size settings, contrast settings, textual alternatives to images, and Web features such as frames, links, and plug-ins.

Screen magnification to enlarge portions of a display or text conversion to Braille or voice output can be done with hardware and software supplied by many vendors. Text-to-speech conversion can help blind users to receive electronic mail or to read text files, and speech-recognition devices permit voice-controlled operation of some software. Graphical user interfaces were a setback for vision-impaired users, but technology innovations from commercial tools such as Freedom Scientific's JAWS, GW Micro's Window-Eyes, or Dolphin's HAL screen readers facilitate conversion of spatial information into nonvisual modes (Poll and Waterham, 1995; Thatcher, 1994; Mynatt and Weber, 1994). Similarly IBM's Home Page Reader and Conversa's Web browser enable access to Web information and services.

Users with hearing impairments generally can use computers with only simple changes (conversion of tones to visual signals is often easy to accomplish) and can benefit from office environments that make heavy use of electronic mail and facsimile transmission (FAX). Telecommunications devices for the deaf (TDD) enable telephone access to information (such as train or airplane schedules) and services (federal agencies and many companies offer TDD access). Special input devices for users with physical disabilities will depend on the user's specific impairment; numerous assistive devices are available. Speech recognition, eye-gaze control, head-mounted optical mice, and many other innovative devices (even the telephone) were pioneered for the needs of disabled users (see Chapter 9).

Designers can benefit by planning early to accommodate users who have disabilities, since at this point substantial improvements can be made at low or no cost. The term *computer curbcuts* brings up the image of sidewalk cutouts to permit wheelchair access, which are cheaper to build than standard curbs if they are planned in advance rather than added later. Similarly, moving the on/off switch to the front of a computer adds a minimal charge, if any, to the cost of manufacturing, but it improves ease of use for all users, and especially for the mobility-impaired.

The motivation to accommodate users who have disabilities has increased since the enactment of U.S. Public Laws 99–506 and 100–542, which require U.S. government agencies to establish accessible information environments that accommodate employees and citizens who have disabilities. Any company wishing to sell products to the U.S. government should adhere to these requirements. Further information about accommodation in workplaces, schools, and the home is available from many sources:

- Private foundations (e.g., the American Foundation for the Blind and the National Federation of the Blind)
- Associations (e.g., the Alexander Graham Bell Association for the Deaf, the National Association for the Deaf, and the Blinded Veterans Association)
- Government agencies (e.g., the National Library Service for the Blind and Physically Handicapped of the Library of Congress and the Center for Technology in Human Disabilities at the Maryland Rehabilitation Center)
- University groups (e.g., the Trace Research and Development Center on Communications and the Control and Computer Access for Handicapped Individuals at the University of Wisconsin)
- Manufacturers (e.g., Apple, IBM, and Microsoft)

Learning-disabled children, including dyslexics, account for at least two percent of the school-age population in the United States. Their education can be positively influenced by design of special courseware with limits on lengthy textual instructions, confusing graphics, extensive typing, and difficult presentation formats (Neuman, 1991). Based on observations of 62 students using 26 packages over 5.5 months, Neuman's advice to designers of courseware for learning-disabled students is applicable to all users:

- Present procedures, directions, and verbal content at levels and in formats that make them accessible even to poor readers.
- Ensure that response requirements do not allow students to complete programs without engaging with target concepts.
- Design feedback sequences that explain the reasons for students' errors and that lead students through the processes necessary for responding correctly.
- Incorporate reinforcement techniques that capitalize on students' sophistication with out-of-school electronic materials.

The potential for great benefit to people with disabilities is one of the unfolding gifts of computing. The Association for Computing Machinery (ACM) Special Interest Group on Computers and the Physically Handicapped (SIGCAPH) publishes a newsletter and runs a yearly conference on Assistive Technology (ASSETS).

1.5.6 Elderly users

Most people grow old. There can be many pleasures and satisfactions to seniority, but aging can also have negative physical, cognitive, and social consequences. Understanding the human factors of aging can lead us to computer designs that will facilitate access by the elderly. The benefits to the elderly include meeting practical needs for writing, accounting, and the full range of computer tools, plus the satisfactions of education, entertainment, social interaction, communication, and challenge (Furlong and Kearsley, 1990). Other benefits include increased access of society to the elderly for their experience, increased participation of the elderly in society through communication networks, and improved chances for productive employment of the elderly.

The National Research Council's report on Human Factors Research Needs for an Aging Population describes aging as

> A nonuniform set of progressive changes in physiological and psychological functioning.... Average visual and auditory acuity decline considerably with age, as do average strength and speed of response.... [People experience] loss of at least some kinds of memory function, declines in perceptual flexibility, slowing of "stimulus encoding," and increased difficulty in the acquisition of complex mental skills,... visual functions such as static visual acuity, dark adaptation, accommodation, contrast sensitivity, and peripheral vision decline, on average, with age. (Czaja, 1990)

This list has its discouraging side, but many people experience only modest effects and continue participating in many activities, even through their nineties.

The further good news is that computer-systems designers can do much to accommodate elderly users, and thus to give the elderly access to the beneficial aspects of computing and network communication. How many young people's lives might be enriched by electronic-mail access to grandparents or great-grandparents? How many businesses might benefit from electronic consultations with experienced senior citizens? How many government agencies, universities, medical centers, or law firms could advance their goals by easily available contact with knowledgeable elderly citizens? As a society, how might we all benefit from the continued creative work of senior citizens in literature, art, music, science, or philosophy?

As the world population grows older, designers in many fields are adapting their work to serve the elderly. Larger street signs, brighter traffic lights, and better nighttime lighting can make driving safer for drivers and pedestrians. Similarly, larger fonts, higher display contrast, easier-to-use pointing devices, louder audio tones, and simpler command languages are just a few of the steps that user-interface designers can take to improve access for the elderly (Czaja and Lee, 2002). Many of these adjustments can be made through software-based control panels that enable users to tailor the system to their changing personal needs. System developers have yet to venture actively into the potentially profitable world of golden-age software, in parallel to the growing market in kidware. Let's do it *before* Bill Gates turns 65!

Electronic-networking projects, such as the San Francisco–based SeniorNet, are providing adults 50+ with access to and education about computing and the Internet "to enhance their lives and enable them to share their knowledge and wisdom." Computer games are also attractive for the elderly because they stimulate social interaction, provide practice in sensorimotor skills such as eye-hand coordination, enhance dexterity, and improve reaction time. In addition, meeting a challenge and gaining a sense of accomplishment and mastery are helpful in improving self-image for anyone (Whitcomb, 1990).

In our research group's brief experiences in bringing computing to two residences for elderly people, we also found that the users' widespread fear of computers and belief that they were incapable of using computers gave way quickly with a few positive experiences. These elderly users, who explored spreadsheets, word processors, and educational games, felt quite satisfied with themselves, were eager to learn more, and transferred their new-found enthusiasm to trying automated bank machines or supermarket touchscreen computers. Suggestions for redesigns to meet the needs of elderly users (and possibly other users) also emerged—for example, the appeal of high-precision touchscreens compared with the mouse (see Chapter 9).

In summary, computing for elderly users provides an opportunity for the elderly, for system developers, and for all society. For more information on this topic, check out the Human Factors & Ergonomics Society, whichhas a Technical Group on Aging that publishes a newsletter and organizes sessions at conferences.

1.5.7 Designing for and with children

Another lively community of users is children, whose uses emphasize entertainment and education. Even pre-readers can use computer-controlled toys, music generators, and art tools. As they mature to begin reading and gain limited keyboard skills, they can use a wider array of portable devices, desktop applications, and Web services. When they become teenagers, they may become highly proficient users who often help their parents or other adults. This idealized growth path is followed by many children who have easy access to technology and supportive parents and peers. However, many children without financial resources or supportive learning environments struggle to gain access to technology. They are often frustrated with its use and are endangered by threats surrounding privacy, alienation, pornography, unhelpful peers, and malevolent strangers.

The noble aspirations of developers of children's software include educational acceleration, socialization with peers, and the positive self-image or self-confidence that comes from mastery of skills. Advocates of educational games promote intrinsic motivation and constructive activities as goals, but opponents often complain about the harmful effects of antisocial and violent games (Future of Children, 2000).

For teenagers, the opportunities for empowerment are substantial. They often take the lead in employing new modes of communication and creating cultural or fashion trends that surprise even the developers, such as instant messaging, text messaging on cell phones, playing with simulations and fantasy games, and exploring Web-based virtual worlds.

Appropriate design principles for children's software recognize young people's intense desire for the kind of interactive engagement that gives them control with appropriate feedback and supports their social engagement with peers (Druin and Inkpen, 2002; Bruckman and Bandlow, 2002). Designers also have to find the balance between children's desire for challenge, and parents requirements for safety. Children can deal with some frustrations and with threatening stories, but they also want to know that they can clear the screen, start over, and try again without severe penalties. They don't easily tolerate patronizing comments or inappropriate humor, but they like familiar characters, exploratory environments, and the capacity for repetition. Younger children will sometimes replay a game, reread a story, or replay a music sequence dozens of times, even after adults have tired. Some designers work by observing children and testing software with children, while the innovative approach of "children as our technology-design partners" engages children in a long-term process of cooperative inquiry during which children and adults jointly design novel products and services (Druin *et al.*, 1999).

Designing for younger children requires attention to their limitations. Their limited dexterity means that mouse dragging, double-clicking, or small targets cannot be used; their lack of literacy means that instructions and error messages are not effective; and their low capacity for abstraction means that complex sequences must be avoided unless an adult is involved. Other concerns are short attention spans and limited capacity to work with multiple concepts simultaneously. Designers of children's software also have a responsibility to attend to dangers, especially in Web-based environments, where parental control over access to violent, racist, or pornographic materials is unfortunately necessary. Appropriate education of children about privacy issues and threats from strangers is also a requirement.

The capacity for playful creativity in art, music, and writing, as well as educational activities in science and math remain potent reasons to pursue children's software. Enabling them to make high-quality images, photos, songs, or poems, and then share them with friends and family, can accelerate children's personal and social development. Offering access to educational materials from libraries, museums, government agencies, schools, and commercial sources enriches their learning experiences and serves as a basis for children to construct their own Web resources, participate in collaborative efforts, and contribute to community-service projects. Providing programming and simulation building tools enables older children to take on complex cognitive challenges and construct ambitious artifacts for others to use.

1.5.8 Accommodating hardware and software diversity

In addition to accommodating different classes of users and skill levels, designers need to support a wide range of hardware and software platforms. The rapid progress of technology means that newer systems may have a hundred or a thousand times greater storage capacity, faster processors, and higher-bandwidth networks. Designers need to accommodate older devices and deal with newer portable devices that may have low-bandwidth connections and small screens. The challenge of accommodating diverse hardware is coupled with the need to ensure access through many generations of software. New operating systems, Web browsers, e-mail clients, and application programs should provide backward compatibility in user-interface design and file structures. Skeptics will say that this requirement can slow innovation, but designers who plan ahead carefully to support flexible interfaces and self-defining files will be rewarded with larger market shares (Shneiderman, 2000).

For at least the next decade, three of the main technical challenges will be:

- Producing satisfying and effective Internet interaction on high-speed (broadband) and slower (dial-up and some wireless) connections. Some technology breakthroughs have already been made in compression algorithms to reduce file sizes for images, music, animations, and even video, but more are needed. New technologies are needed to enable pre-fetch or scheduled downloads and better cacheing strategies. User control of the amount of material downloaded for each request could also prove beneficial (for example, allowing users to specify that a large image should be reduced to a smaller size, sent with fewer colors, converted to a simplified line drawing, or even replaced with just a text description).
- Enabling access to Web services from large display devices (1200 × 1600 pixels or larger) and smaller ones (640 × 480 and smaller). Rewriting each Web page for different display sizes may produce the best quality, but this approach is probably too costly and time consuming for most Web providers. New software-tool breakthroughs are needed to allow Web-site developers to specify their content in such a way that automatic conversions can be made for an increasing range of display sizes.
- Supporting easy maintenance of or automatic conversion to multiple languages. Commercial operators recognize that they can expand their markets if they can provide access in multiple languages and across multiple countries. This means isolating text to allow easy substitution, choosing appropriate metaphors and colors, and addressing the needs of diverse cultures (see Section 1.5.4).

The good news is that rethinking designs to accommodate these diverse needs can improve the quality for all users. As for costs, with appropriate software tools, e-commerce providers are finding that a small additional effort can expand markets by as much as 20% or more.

1.6 Goals for Our Profession

Clear goals are useful not only for system development but also for educational and professional enterprises. Three broad goals seem attainable:

(1) influencing academic and industrial researchers; (2) providing tools, techniques, and knowledge for commercial systems implementers; and (3) raising the computer consciousness of the general public.

1.6.1 Influencing academic and industrial researchers

Early research in human-computer interaction was done largely by introspection and intuition, but this approach suffered from lack of validity, generality, and precision. The techniques of controlled, psychologically oriented experimentation can lead to a deeper understanding of the fundamental principles of human interaction with computers.

The reductionist scientific method has this basic outline:

- Understanding of a practical problem and related theory
- Lucid statement of a testable hypothesis
- Manipulation of a small number of independent variables
- Measurement of specific dependent variables
- Careful selection and assignment of subjects
- Control for bias in subjects, procedures, and materials
- Application of statistical tests
- Interpretation of results, refinement of theory, and guidance for experimenters

Materials and methods must be tested by pilot experiments, and results must be validated by replication in variant situations.

Of course, the highly developed and structured method of controlled experimentation has its weaknesses. It may be difficult or expensive to find adequate subjects, and laboratory conditions may distort the situation so much that the conclusions have no application. When we arrive at results for large groups of subjects by statistical aggregation, extremely good or poor performance by individuals may be overlooked. Furthermore, anecdotal evidence or individual insights may be given too little emphasis because of the authoritative influence of statistics.

In spite of these concerns, controlled experimentation provides a productive basis that can be modified to suit the situation. Anecdotal experiences and subjective reactions should be recorded, thinking aloud or protocol approaches should be employed, field or case studies with extensive performance data collection should be carried out, and the individual insights of researchers, designers, and experimental participants should be captured.

Within computer science, there is a growing awareness of the need for greater attention to human-factors issues. Researchers who propose new programming languages, privacy-protection schemes, or network services are more aware of the need to match human cognitive skills. Developers of advanced graphics systems, agile manufacturing equipment, or computer-assisted design systems increasingly recognize that the success of their proposals depends on the construction of a suitable human interface. Researchers in these and other areas are making efforts to understand and measure human performance.

There is a grand opportunity to apply the knowledge and techniques of traditional psychology (and of subfields such as cognitive psychology) to the study of human-computer interaction. Psychologists are investigating human problem solving and creativity with computers to gain an understanding of cognitive processes. The benefit to psychology is great, but psychologists also have a golden opportunity to influence dramatically an important and widely used technology.

Researchers in information science, business and management, education, sociology, anthropology, and other disciplines are benefiting and contributing by their study of human-computer interaction (National Research Council, 1983; Marchionini and Sibert, 1991). There are so many fruitful directions for research that any list can be only a provocative starting point. Here are a few:

- *Reduced anxiety and fear of computer usage.* Although computers are widely used, they still serve only a fraction of the population. Many otherwise competent people resist use of computers. Some elderly users avoid helpful computer-based devices, such as bank terminals or word processors, because they are anxious about—or even fearful of—breaking the computer or making an embarrassing mistake. Interviews with nonusers of computers would help us to determine the sources of this anxiety and to formulate design guidelines for alleviating the fear. Tests could be run to determine the effectiveness of the redesigned systems and of improved training procedures.
- *Graceful evolution.* Although novices may begin their interactions with a computer by using menu selection, they may wish to evolve to faster or more powerful facilities. Methods are needed to smooth the transition from novice to knowledgeable user to expert. The differing requirements of novices and experts in prompting, error messages, online assistance, display complexity, locus of control, pacing, and informative feedback all need investigation. The design of control panels to support customization is also an open topic.

- *Specification and implementation of interaction.* User-interface–building tools (discussed in Chapter 5) reduce implementation times by an order of magnitude when they match the task. There are still many situations in which extensive coding in procedural languages must be added. Advanced research on tools to aid interactive-systems designers and implementers might have substantial payoffs in reducing costs and improving quality. For example, tools for World Wide Web designers to enable automatic conversion for different computers, screen sizes, or modem speeds could be substantially improved, thereby facilitating universal usability.
- *Direct manipulation.* Visual interfaces in which users operate on a representation of the objects of interest are extremely attractive (see Chapter 6). Empirical studies could refine our understanding of appropriate analogical or metaphorical representations and of the role of rapid, incremental, reversible operations. Newer forms of direct manipulation—such as visual languages, information visualization, telepresence, and virtual reality—are further topics for research.
- *Input devices.* The plethora of input devices presents opportunities and challenges to system designers (see Chapter 6). There are heated discussions about the relative merits of the high-precision touchscreen; stylus, voice, eye-gaze, and gestural input; the mouse; and haptic devices. Such conflicts could be resolved through experimentation with multiple tasks and users. Underlying issues include speed, accuracy, fatigue, error correction, and subjective satisfaction.
- *Online assistance.* Although many systems offer some help or tutorial information online, we have only limited understanding of what constitutes effective design for novices, knowledgeable users, and experts (see Chapter 12). The role of these aids and of online user communities could be studied to assess effects on user success and satisfaction.
- *Information exploration.* As navigation, browsing, and searching of multimedia digital libraries and the World Wide Web become more common, the pressure for more effective strategies and tools will increase (see Chapter 15). Users will want to filter, select, and restructure their information rapidly and with minimum effort, without fear of disorientation or of getting lost. Large databases of text, images, graphics, sound, and scientific data will become easier to explore with emerging information-visualization tools.

1.6.2 Providing tools, techniques, and knowledge for systems implementers

User-interface design and development are currently hot topics, and international competition is lively. There is a great thirst for knowledge, software tools, design guidelines, and testing techniques. New user-interface–building tools (see Chapter 5) provide support for rapid prototyping and system development while aiding design consistency and simplifying evolutionary refinement.

Guidelines documents have been written for general and specific audiences. Many projects are taking the productive route of writing their own guidelines, which are tied to the problems of their application environments. These guidelines are constructed from experimental results, experience with existing systems, and knowledgeable guesswork.

Iterative usability studies and acceptance testing are appropriate during system development. Once the initial system is available, refinements can be made on the basis of online or printed surveys, individual or group interviews, or more controlled empirical tests of novel strategies (see Chapter 4).

Feedback from users during the development process and for evolutionary refinement can provide useful insights and guidance. Online electronic-mail facilities allow users to send comments directly to the designers. Online user consultants and fellow users can provide prompt assistance and supportive encouragement.

1.6.3 Raising the computer consciousness of the general public

The media are so filled with stories about computers that raising public consciousness of these tools may seem unnecessary. In fact, however, many people are still uncomfortable with computers. When they do finally use a bank machine or word processor, they may be fearful of making mistakes, anxious about damaging the equipment, worried about feeling incompetent, or threatened by the computer "being smarter than I am." These fears are generated, in part, by poor designs that have complex commands, hostile and vague error messages, tortuous and unfamiliar sequences of actions, or a deceptive anthropomorphic style.

One of my goals is to encourage users to translate their internal fears into outraged action (Shneiderman, 2002). Instead of feeling guilty when they get a message such as SYNTAX ERROR, users should express their anger at the system designer who was so inconsiderate and thoughtless. Instead of feeling inadequate or foolish because they cannot remember a complex sequence of actions, they should complain to the designer who did not provide a more convenient mechanism or should seek another product that does.

Usability ultimately becomes a question of national priorities, as advocates of electronic voting and other services, promoters of e-healthcare, and visionaries of e-learning increasingly influence allocation of government resources. Policymakers and industry leaders become heroes in making appropriate technology decisions and villains when failures threaten children, disrupt travel, or menace consumers.

As examples of successful and satisfying systems become more visible, the crude designs will appear increasingly archaic and will become commercial failures. As designers improve interactive systems, some of these fears will recede and the positive experiences of competence, mastery, and satisfaction will flow in. Then, the images of computer scientists and system designers will change in the public's view. The machine-oriented and technical image will give way to one of personal warmth, sensitivity, and concern for the user.

1.7 Practitioner's Summary

If you are designing an interactive system, a thorough task analysis can provide the information for a proper functional design. You should pay attention to reliability, availability, security, integrity, standardization, portability, integration, and the administrative issues of schedules and budgets. As design alternatives are proposed, they can be evaluated for their role in providing short learning times, rapid task performance, low error rates, ease of retention, and high user satisfaction. As the design is refined and implemented, you can test for accomplishment of these goals with pilot studies, expert reviews, usability tests, user observations, and acceptance tests. The rapidly growing literature and sets of design guidelines may be of assistance in developing your project standards and practices and in accommodating the increasingly diverse and growing community of users.

WORLD WIDE WEB RESOURCES

This book is accompanied by an extensive Web site (http://www.aw.com/DTUI/) prepared by Jennifer Pelland at Addison-Wesley, that includes pointers to additional resources tied to the contents of each chapter. In addition, this Web site contains information for instructors, students, practitioners, and researchers. The links for Chapter 1 include general resources on human-computer interaction, such as professional societies, government agencies, companies, bibliographies, and guidelines documents.

People seeking references to scientific journals and conferences now have an online searchable bibliography for human–computer interaction (http://www.hcibib.org/). Built under the heroic leadership of Gary Perlman, it makes available almost 25,000 journal, conference, and book abstracts.

Three wonderful sets of pointers to World Wide Web resources are:

1. Diamond Bullet Design (http://www.usabilityfirst.com/)
2. HCI Index (http://degraaff.org/hci/)
3. Usability and Beyond (http://www15.brinkster.com/stijn-scholts/links/default.asp)

Excellent electronic mailing lists for announcements and discussion lists are maintained by ACM SIGCHI (http://www.acm.org/ sigchi/) and by the British HCI Group (http://www.bcs-hci.org.uk/).

http://www.aw.com/DTUI

1.8 Researcher's Agenda

The opportunities for researchers are unlimited. There are so many interesting, important, and doable projects that it may be hard to choose a direction. Each experiment has two parents: the practical problems facing designers, and the fundamental theories based on principles of human behavior and interface design. Begin by proposing a lucid, testable hypothesis. Then consider the appropriate research methodology, conduct the experiment, collect the data, and analyze the results. Each experiment also has three children: specific recommendations for the practical problem, refinements of your theories, and guidance to future experimenters. Each chapter of this book ends with specific research proposals.

References

Specialized references for this chapter appear here; general information resources are given in the following section.

Bruckman, Amy and Bandlow, Alisa, HCI for Kids, in Jacko, Julie and Sears, Andrew (Editors), *Handbook of Human-Computer Interaction*, Lawrence Erlbaum Associates, Hillsdale, NJ (2002).

Center for Information Technology Accommodation, Section 508: The road to accessibility, General Services Administration, Washington, DC (2002). Available at http://www.section508.gov/index.cfm.

Czaja, S. J. and Lee, C. C., Designing computer systems for older adults, in Jacko, Julie and Sears, Andrew (Editors), *Handbook of Human-Computer Interaction*, Lawrence Erlbaum Associates, Hillsdale, NJ (2002).

Czaja, Sara J. (Editor), *Human Factors Research Needs for an Aging Population*, National Academy Press, Washington, DC (1990).

Druin, Allison and Inkpen, Kori, When personal technologies are for children, *Personal Technologies* 5 (3), (2001), 191–194.

Druin, Allison, *et al.*, Children as our technology design partners, in Druin, Allison (Editor), *Children as Our Technology Design Partners*, Morgan Kaufmann Publishers, San Francisco, CA (1999).

Edwards, Alistair D.N., *Extra-Ordinary Human-Computer Interaction: Interfaces for Users with Disabilities*, Cambridge University Press, Cambridge, UK (1995).

Furlong, Mary and Kearsley, Greg, *Computers for Kids Over 60*, SeniorNet, San Francisco, CA (1990).

Future of Children 10 (2), Special Issue on *Children and Computer Technology*, David and Lucille Packard Foundation, Los Altos, CA (Fall/Winter 2000).

Huff, C. W. and Cooper, J., Sex bias in educational software: The effect of designers' stereotypes on the software they design, *Journal of Applied Social Psychology*, 17, 6 (June 1987), 519–532.

Keirsey, David, *Please Understand Me II: Temperament, Character, Intelligence*, Prometheus Nemesis Books, Del Mar, CA (1998).

Marcus, Aaron and Gould, Emile West, Cultural dimensions and global user-interface design: What? So What? Now What?, *Proc. 6th Conference on Human Factors and the Web* (2000), Available at http://www.tri.sbc.com/hfweb/.

Marchionini, Gary, Ashley, Maryle, and Korzendorfer, Lois, ACCESS at the Library of Congress, in Shneiderman, Ben (Editor), *Sparks of Innovation in Human-Computer Interaction*, Ablex, Norwood, NJ (1993), 251–258.

Marchionini, Gary and Sibert, John (Editors), An agenda for human-computer interaction: Science and engineering serving human needs, *ACM SIGCHI Bulletin* (October 1991), 17–32.

Mynatt, Elizabeth D. and Weber, Gerhard, Nonvisual presentation of graphical user interfaces: Contrasting two approaches, *CHI '94 Human Factors in Computer Systems*, ACM, New York (1994), 166–172.

National Research Council Committee on Human Factors, *Research Needs in Human Factors*, National Academy Press, Washington, DC (1983).

Neuman, Delia, Learning disabled students' interactions with commercial courseware: A naturalistic study, *Educational Technology Research and Development*, 39, 1 (1991), 31–49.

Poll, Leonard H. D. and Waterham, Ronald P., Graphical user interfaces and visually disabled users, *IEEE Transactions on Rehabilitation Engineering*, 3, 1 (March 1995), 65–69.

Thatcher, James W., Screen Reader/2: Access to OS/2 and the graphical user interface, *Proc. ACM SIGCAPH—Computers and the Physically Handicapped, ASSETS '94* (1994), 39–47.

Vanderheiden, Greg, Fundamental principles and priority setting for universal usability, *Proc. ACM Conference on Universal Usability*, ACM, New York (2000), 32–38.

Whitcomb, G. Robert, Computer games for the elderly, *Proc. Conference on Computers and the Quality of Life '90*, ACM SIGCAS, New York (1990), 112–115.

General information resources

Primary journals include the following:

ACM Transactions on Computer-Human Interaction, ACM, New York.

ACM Interactions: A Magazine for User Interface Designers, ACM, New York.

Behaviour & Information Technology (BIT), Taylor & Francis Ltd., London, UK.

Computer Supported Cooperative Work, Kluwer Academic Publishers, Dordecht, The Netherlands.

Human-Computer Interaction, Lawrence Erlbaum Associates, Hillsdale, NJ.

Information Visualization, Palgrave Macmillan, Houndmills, Basingstoke, UK.

Interacting with Computers, Butterworth Heinemann Ltd., Oxford, UK.

International Journal of Human-Computer Studies, formerly *International Journal of Man-Machine Studies (IJMMS)*, Academic Press, London, UK.

International Journal of Human-Computer Interaction, Lawrence Erlbaum Associates, Hillsdale, NJ.

Other journals that regularly carry articles of interest include:

ACM Computing Surveys

Communications of the ACM (CACM)

ACM Transactions on Graphics

ACM Transactions on Information Systems

Cognitive Science

Computers and Human Behavior

Ergonomics

Human Factors (HF)

IEEE Computer

IEEE Computer Graphics and Applications

IEEE Software

IEEE Transactions on Systems, Man, and Cybernetics (IEEE SMC)

Journal of Visual Languages and Computing

UMUAI: User Modeling and User-Adapted Interaction

The Association for Computing Machinery (ACM) Special Interest Group on Computer & Human Interaction (SIGCHI) publishes a newsletter and holds regularly scheduled conferences. Other ACM Special Interest Groups, such as Graphics (SIGGRAPH), Computers and the Physically Handicapped (SIGCAPH), and hypertext plus multimedia (SIGLINK), also produce conferences and newsletters. The American Society for Information Science & Technology (ASIST) has a Special Interest Group on Human-Computer Interaction (SIGHCI) that publishes a newsletter and organizes sessions at the annual ASIST convention. The Human Factors & Ergonomics Society has a Computer Systems Technical Group with a newsletter. The International Federation for Information Processing has a Technical Committee and Working Groups on human-computer interaction. The British Computer Society Human-Computer Interaction Group, French Association Francais pour l'Interaction Homme-Machine (AFIHM), and other national groups promote development within their countries.

Conferences—such as the ones held by the ACM (especially SIGCHI and SIGGRAPH), IEEE, ASIST, Human Factors & Ergonomics Society, and IFIP—often have relevant papers presented and published in the proceedings. INTERACT, Human-Computer Interaction International, and the Work with Display Units series of conferences (held approximately every other year) are also important resources with broad coverage of user-interface issues. Several more specialized ACM conferences may also be of interest: User Interfaces Software and Technology, Hypertext, Computer-Supported Cooperative Work, Intelligent User Interfaces, Universal Usability, Computers and Cognition, Designing Interactive Systems, etc. The Association for Information Systems (AIS) now has a Special Interest Group in Human-Computer Interaction related to business and management.

The following list of guidelines documents and books is a starting point to the large and growing literature in this area. Gerald Weinberg's 1971 book, *The Psychology of Computer Programming,* is a continuing inspiration to thinking about how people interact with computers. James Martin provided a thoughtful and useful survey of interactive systems in his 1973 book, *Design of Man-Computer Dialogues.* My 1980 book, *Software Psychology: Human Factors in Computer and Information Systems,* promoted the use of controlled experimental techniques and the reductionist scientific method. Rubinstein and Hersh's *The Human Factor: Designing Computer Systems for People* (1984) offered an appealing introduction to computer-system design and many useful guidelines. The first edition of this book, published in 1987, reviewed critical issues, offered guidelines for designers, and suggested research directions.

Don Norman's 1988 book, *The Psychology of Everyday Things,* is a refreshing look at the psychological issues in the design of the everyday technology that surrounds us. As a reader, I was provoked equally by the sections dealing with doors or showers and computers or calculators. This book has a wonderful blend of levity and great depth of thinking, practical wisdom, and thoughtful theory.

A steady flow of influential books during the 1990s included Hix and Hartson's *Developing User Interfaces* (1993), Nielsen's *Usability Engineering* (1993), Preece *et al.*'s *Human-Computer Interaction* (1994), and Landauer's *The Trouble with Computers* (1995). Recent recommended books include Nielsen's *Designing Web Usability: The Practice of Simplicity*; Preece, Rogers, and Sharp's *Interaction Design*; and Norman's *The Invisible Computer.*

An important development for the field was the creation (in 1991) of a professional group, the Usability Professionals Association, and their new magazine, called *User Experience.* 1994 marked the appearance of ACM's professional magazine, entitled *interactions,* and academic journal, *Transactions on Computer-Human Interaction.* As the field matures, specialized topics form their own subgroups and publications, as is happening with mobile computing, Web design, online communities, information visualization, etc.

Guidelines documents

Apple Aqua Human Interface Guidelines, Apple, Cupertino, CA (2002).

—Explains how to design interfaces for Mac OS X.

Apple Computer, Inc., *Macintosh Human Interface Guidelines,* Addison-Wesley, Reading, MA (1992).

—A beautifully produced color book. A well-designed CD-ROM, *Making it Macintosh,* exemplifies these Mac guidelines (Addison-Wesley, Reading, MA, 1993).

BSR/HFES Human Factors Engineering of Computer Workstations (Draft Standard), Human Factors Society, Santa Monica, CA (March 2002).

—Carefully considered revised standards for the design, installation, and use of computer workstations. Emphasizes ergonomics and anthropometrics.

Human Engineering Design Criteria for Military Systems, Equipment and Facilities, Military Standard MIL-STD–1472F, U.S. Government Printing Office, Washington, DC (1999).

—Covers traditional ergonomic and anthropometric issues. Later editions pay increasing attention to user-computer interfaces. Interesting and thought-provoking reminder of many human-factors issues.

International Organisation for Standardisation, *ISO9241 Ergonomic Requirements for Office Work with Visual Display Terminals (VDTs), Part 11: Guidance on Usability*, Geneva, Switzerland (1998). *ISO16071 Ergonomics of Human-System Interaction - Guidance on Software Accessibility*, Technical Specification, Geneva, Switzerland, (2002). Available from American National Standards Institute, 11 West 42nd Street, New York, NY.

—General introduction, dialog principles, guidance on usability, presentation of information, user guidance, menu dialogs, command dialogs, direct-manipulation dialogs, form-filling dialogs.

Microsoft, Inc., *The Microsoft Windows User Experience*, Microsoft Press, Redmond, WA (1999).

Microsoft, Inc., *Windows XP Visual Guidelines*, Microsoft Press, Redmond, WA (2001).

—Thoughtful analysis of usability principles (user in control, directness, consistency, forgiveness, aesthetics, and simplicity) gives detailed guidance for Windows software developers regarding how to make it happen. The guidelines for Windows XP emphasize simplicity, color, freshness, and excitement.

NASA User-Interface Guidelines, Goddard Space Flight Center-Code 520, Greenbelt, MD (January 1996). Available at http://aaaprod.gsfc.nasa.gov/usability/use/UG_96/.

—The purpose of this document is to present user-interface guidelines that specifically address graphic and object-oriented interfaces operating in either distributed or independent systems environments. Principles and general guidelines are given, with many graphic-interface examples for a variety of platforms.

Smith, Sid L. and Mosier, Jane N., *Guidelines for Designing User Interface Software*, Report ESD-TR-86-278, Electronic Systems Division, MITRE Corporation, Bedford, MA (August 1986). Available from National Technical Information Service, Springfield, VA.

—This thorough document, which has undergone several revisions, begins with a good discussion of human-factors issues in design. It then covers data entry, data display, and sequence control. Guidelines are offered with comments, examples, exceptions, and references. This report is *the* place to start if you are creating your own guidelines.

Sun Microsystems, Inc., *Java Look and Feel Design Guidelines*, Addison-Wesley, Reading, MA (1999).

—Shows designers how to create visual design and behaviors in a consistent, compatible, and aesthetic manner.

World Wide Web Consortium's Web Accessibility Initiative, *Web content accessibility guidelines 1.0*, Geneva, Switzerland (1999). Available at http://www.w3.org/TR/WAI-WEBCONTENT/.

World Wide Web Consortium's Web Accessibility Initiative, *Evaluation, repair, and transformation tools for web content accessibility*, Geneva, Switzerland (2002). Available at http://www.w3.org/WAI/ER/existingtools.html.

Books

Classic books

Bolt, Richard A., *The Human Interface: Where People and Computers Meet*, Lifelong Learning Publications, Belmont, CA (1984), 113 pages.

Brown, C. Marlin "Lin," *Human-Computer Interface Design Guidelines*, Ablex, Norwood, NJ (1988), 236 pages.

Cakir, A., Hart, D. J., and Stewart, T. F. M., *Visual Display Terminals: A Manual Covering Ergonomics, Workplace Design, Health and Safety, Task Organization*, John Wiley & Sons, New York (1980).

Card, Stuart K., Moran, Thomas P., and Newell, Allen, *The Psychology of Human-Computer Interaction*, Lawrence Erlbaum Associates, Hillsdale, NJ (1983), 469 pages.

Carroll, John M., *The Nurnberg Funnel: Designing Minimalist Instruction for Practical Computer Skill*, MIT Press, Cambridge, MA (1990), 340 pages.

Crawford, Chris, *The Art of Computer Game Design: Reflections of a Master Game Designer*, Osborne/McGraw-Hill, Berkeley, CA (1984), 113 pages.

Dreyfus, W., *The Measure of Man: Human Factors in Design, Second Edition*, Whitney Library of Design, New York (1967).

Duffy, Thomas M., Palmer, James E., and Mehlenbacher, Brad, *Online Help: Design and Evaluation*, Ablex, Norwood, NJ (1993), 260 pages.

Eberts, Ray E., *User Interface Design*, Prentice-Hall, Englewood Cliffs, NJ (1993), 649 pages.

Ehrich, R. W. and Williges, R. C., *Human-Computer Dialogue Design*, Elsevier Science Publishers B.V., Amsterdam, The Netherlands (1986).

Foley, James D., van Dam, Andries, Feiner, Steven K., and Hughes, John F., *Computer Graphics: Principles and Practice, Second Edition*, Addison-Wesley, Reading, MA (1990), 1174 pages.

Hiltz, Starr Roxanne, *Online Communities: A Case Study of the Office of the Future*, Ablex, Norwood, NJ (1984), 261 pages.

Hiltz, Starr Roxanne and Turoff, Murray, *The Network Nation: Human Communication via Computer*, Addison-Wesley, Reading, MA (1978, revised edition 1998).

Hix, Deborah, and Hartson, H. Rex, *Developing User Interfaces: Ensuring Usability Through Product and Process*, John Wiley & Sons, New York (1993), 381 pages.

Kantowitz, Barry H. and Sorkin, Robert D., *Human Factors: Understanding People-System Relationships*, John Wiley & Sons, New York (1983), 699 pages.

Kearsley, Greg, *Online Help Systems: Design and Implementation*, Ablex, Norwood, NJ (1988), 115 pages.

Krueger, Myron, *Artificial Reality II*, Addison-Wesley, Reading, MA (1991), 304 pages.

Laurel, Brenda, *Computers as Theater*, Addison-Wesley, Reading, MA (1991), 211 pages.

Marcus, Aaron, *Graphic Design for Electronic Documents and User Interfaces*, ACM Press, New York (1992), 266 pages.

Martin, James, *Design of Man-Computer Dialogues*, Prentice-Hall, Englewood Cliffs, NJ (1973), 509 pages.

Mumford, Enid, *Designing Human Systems for New Technology*, Manchester Business School, Manchester, UK (1983), 108 pages.

National Research Council, Committee on Human Factors, *Research Needs for Human Factors*, National Academy Press, Washington, DC (1983), 160 pages.

Nickerson, Raymond S., *Using Computers: Human Factors in Information Systems*, MIT Press, Cambridge, MA (1986), 434 pages.

Nielsen, Jakob, *Usability Engineering*, Academic Press, Boston, MA (1993), 358 pages.

Norman, Donald A., *The Psychology of Everyday Things*, Basic Books, New York (1988), 257 pages.

Norman, Kent, *The Psychology of Menu Selection: Designing Cognitive Control at the Human/Computer Interface*, Ablex, Norwood, NJ (1991), 350 pages.

Preece, Jenny, *A Guide to Usability: Human Factors in Computing*, Addison-Wesley, Reading, MA (1993), 144 pages.

Pheasant, Stephen, *Bodyspace: Anthropometry, Ergonomics and the Design of the Work, Second Edition*, Taylor & Francis, London, UK (1996).

Rubinstein, Richard and Hersh, Harry, *The Human Factor: Designing Computer Systems for People*, Digital Press, Maynard, MA (1984), 249 pages.

Sanders, M. S. and McCormick, Ernest J., *Human Factors in Engineering and Design, Seventh Edition*, McGraw-Hill, New York (1993).

Sheridan, T. B. and Ferrel, W. R., *Man-Machine Systems: Information, Control, and Decision Models of Human Performance*, MIT Press, Cambridge, MA (1974).

Shneiderman, Ben, *Software Psychology: Human Factors in Computer and Information Systems*, Little, Brown, Boston, MA (1980), 320 pages.

Shneiderman, Ben and Kearsley, Greg, *Hypertext Hands-On! An Introduction to a New Way of Organizing and Accessing Information*, Addison-Wesley, Reading, MA (1989), 165 pages and two disks.

Thimbleby, Harold, *User Interface Design*, ACM Press, New York (1990), 470 pages.

Thorell, L. G. and Smith, W. J., *Using Computer Color Effectively*, Prentice-Hall, Englewood Cliffs, NJ (1990., 258 pages.

Tognazzini, Bruce, *Tog on Interface*, Addison-Wesley, Reading, MA (1992), 331 pages.

Travis, David, *Effective Color Displays: Theory and Practice*, Academic Press, Harcourt Brace Jovanovich, London, UK (1991), 301 pages.

Turkle, Sherry, *The Second Self: Computers and the Human Spirit*, Simon and Schuster, New York (1984).

Vaske, Jerry and Grantham, Charles, *Socializing the Human-Computer Environment*, Ablex, Norwood, NJ (1990), 290 pages.

Weinberg, Gerald M., *The Psychology of Computer Programming*, Van Nostrand Reinhold, New York (1971), 288 pages.

Weizenbaum, Joseph, *Computer Power and Human Reason: From Judgment to Calculation*, W. H. Freeman, San Francisco, CA (1976), 300 pages.

Winograd, Terry and Flores, Fernando, *Understanding Computers and Cognition*, Ablex, Norwood, NJ (1986), 207 pages.

Zuboff, Shoshanna, *In the Age of the Smart Machine: The Future of Work and Power*, Basic Books, New York (1988), 468 pages.

Recent books

Ashcraft, Mark H., *Cognition, Third Edition*, Prentice-Hall, Englewood Cliffs, NJ (2001), 608 pages.

Bailey, Robert W., *Human Performance Engineering: Using Human Factors/Ergonomics to Achieve Computer Usability, Third Edition*, Prentice-Hall, Englewood Cliffs, NJ (1996), 636 pages.

Beaudouin-Lafon, Michel, *Computer Supported Co-operative Work Trends in Software*, John Wiley & Sons, New York (1999), 258 pages.

Beyer, Hugh and Holtzblatt, Karen, *Contextual Design: Defining Customer-Centered Systems*, Morgan Kaufmann Publishers, San Francisco, CA (1998).

Borchers, Jan, *A Pattern Approach to Interaction Design*, John Wiley & Sons, Chichester, UK (2001), 268 pages.

Carroll, John, M., *Scenario-Based Design: Envisioning Work and Technology in System Development*, John Wiley & Sons, New York (1995), 406 pages.

Carroll, John M., *Making Use: Scenario-Based Design of Human-Computer Interactions*, MIT Press, Cambridge, MA (2000), 382 pages.

Constantine, Larry L. and Lockwood, Lucy A. D., *Software for Use: A Practical Guide to the Models and Methods of Usage-Centered Design*, Addison-Wesley, Reading, MA (1999), 579 pages.

Cooper, Alan, *About Face: The Essentials of User Interface Design, Second Edition*, IDG Books Worldwide, Foster City, CA (2003).

Dix, Alan, Finlay, Janet, Abowd, Gregory, and Beale, Russell, *Human-Computer Interaction, Second Edition*, Prentice-Hall, Englewood, NJ (1998), 650 pages.

Druin, Allison and Solomon, Cynthia, *Designing Multimedia Environments for Children: Computers Creativity and Kids*, John Wiley & Sons, New York (1996), 263 pages.

Dumas, Joseph S. and Redish, Janice C., *A Practical Guide to Usability Testing*, Ablex, Norwood, NJ (1999, revised edition), 304 pages.

Elmes, David G., Kantowitz, Barry H., and Roediger, Henry L., *Research Methods in Psychology, Seventh Edition*, Wadsworth Publishing, Belmont, CA (2002), 655 pages.

Fernandes, Tony, *Global Interface Design: A Guide to Designing International User Interfaces*, Academic Press Professional, Boston, MA (1995), 191 pages.

Galitz, Wilbert O., *The Essential Guide to User Interface Design, Second Edition: An Introduction to GUI Design Principles and Techniques*, John Wiley & Sons, New York (2003).

Hackos, JoAnn T. and Redish, Janice C., *User and Task Analysis for Interface Design*, John Wiley & Sons, New York (1998), 488 pages.

Horton, William K., *Designing and Writing Online Documentation: Hypermedia for Self-Supporting Products*, John Wiley & Sons, New York (1994), 464 pages.

Isaacs, Ellen and Walendowski, Alan, *Designing from Both Sides of the Screen: How Designers and Engineers Can Collaborate to Build Cooperative Technology*, New Riders Publishing, Indianapolis, IN (2001), 352 pages.

Johnson, Jeff, *GUI Bloopers Don'ts and Do's for Software Developers and Web Designers*, Morgan Kaufmann Publishers, San Francisco, CA (2000), 584 pages.

Landauer, Thomas K., *The Trouble with Computers: Usefulness, Usability, and Productivity*, MIT Press, Cambridge, MA (1995), 425 pages.

Mandell, Theo, *The Elements of User Interface Design*, John Wiley & Sons, New York (1997), 440 pages.

Marchionini, Gary, *Information Seeking in Electronic Environments*, Cambridge University Press, Cambridge, UK (1995), 224 pages.

Mayhew, Deborah J., *The Usability Engineering Lifecycle: A Practitioner's Guide to User Interface Design*, Morgan Kaufmann Publishers, San Francisco, CA (1999), 560 pages.

Mullet, Kevin and Sano, Darrell, *Designing Visual Interfaces: Communication Oriented Techniques*, Sunsoft Press, Englewood Cliffs, NJ (1995), 277 pages.

Newman, William M. and Lamming, Michael G., *Interactive Systems Design*, Addison-Wesley, Reading, MA (1995), 468 pages.

Nielsen, Jakob, *Multimedia and Hypertext: The Internet and Beyond*, Academic Press, Cambridge, MA (1995), 480 pages.

Norman, Don, *The Invisible Computer: Why Good Products Can Fail, the Personal Computer Is So Complex, and Information Appliances Are the Solution*, MIT Press, Cambridge, MA (2000), 302 pages.

Olsen, Jr., Dan R., *Developing User Interfaces*, Morgan Kaufmann Publishers, San Francisco, CA (1998), 414 pages.

Preece, Jenny, *Online Communities: Designing Usability and Supporting Sociability*, John Wiley & Sons, New York (2000), 464 pages.

Preece, Jenny, Rogers, Yvonne, Sharp, Helen, Benyon, David, Holland, Simon, and Carey, Tom, *Human-Computer Interaction*, Addison-Wesley, Reading, MA (1994), 773 pages.

Preece, Jenny, Rogers, Yvonne, and Sharp, Helen, *Interaction Design: Beyond Human-Computer Interaction*, John Wiley & Sons, New York, (2002), 544 pages.

Raskin, Jef, *Humane Interface: New Directions for Designing Interactive Systems*, Addison-Wesley, Reading, MA (2000), 256 pages.

Reeves, Byron and Nass, Clifford, *The Media Equation: How People Treat Computers, Television, and New Media Like Real People and Places*, Cambridge University Press, Cambridge, UK (1996).

Rubin, Jeffrey, *Handbook of Usability Testing: How to Plan, Design, and Conduct Effective Tests*, John Wiley & Sons, New York (1994).

Schuler, Douglas, *New Community Networks: Wired for Change*, ACM Press, New York, and Addison-Wesley, Reading, MA (1996), 528 pages.

Shneiderman, Ben, *Leonardo's Laptop: Human Needs and the New Computing Technologies*, MIT Press, Cambridge, MA (2002), 256 pages.

Turkle, Sherry, *Life on the Screen: Identity in the Age of the Internet*, Simon and Schuster, New York (1995).

Ware, Colin, *Information Visualization: Perception for Design*, Morgan Kaufmann Publishers, San Francisco, CA (2000), 384 pages.

Wickens, Christopher D. and Hollands, Justin G., *Engineering Psychology and Human Performance*, Prentice-Hall, Englewood Cliffs, NJ (2000), 573 pages.

Web design books

Alliance for Technology Access, *Computer and Web Resources for People With Disabilities: A Guide to Exploring Today's Assistive Technology*, Hunter House, Alameda, CA (2000), 384 pages.

Brinck, Tom, Gergle, Darren, and Wood, Scott D., *Usability for the Web: Designing Web Sites that Work*, Morgan Kaufmann Publishers, San Francisco, CA (2001), 432 pages.

Cato, John, *User-Centered Web Design*, Addison-Wesley, Reading, MA (2001), 320 pages.

Forsythe, Chris, Grose, Eric, and Ratner, Julie (Editors), *Human Factors and Web Development*, Lawrence Erlbaum Associates, Hillsdale, NJ (1997), 228 pages.

Lazar, Jonathan, *User-Centered Web Development*, Jones & Bartlett Publishers, Boston, MA (2001), 293 pages.

Lynch, Patrick J. and Horton, Sarah, *Web Style Guide: Basic Design Principles for Creating Web Sites*, Yale University Press, New Haven, CT (1999), 164 pages.

Nielsen, Jakob, *Designing Web Usability: The Practice of Simplicity*, New Riders Publishing, Indianapolis, IN (1999), 432 pages.

Nielsen, Jakob and Tahir, Marie, *Homepage Usability: 50 Websites Deconstructed*, New Riders Publishing, Indianapolis, IN (2002), 315 pages.

Paciello, Michael G., *Web Accessibility for People With Disabilities*, CMP Books, Gilroy, CA (2000), 392 pages.

Rosenfeld, Louis and Morville, Peter, *Information Architecture for the World Wide Web*, O'Reilly & Associates, Inc., Sebastopol, CA (1998).

Spool, Jared M., Scanlon, Tara, Schroeder, Will, Snyder, Carolyn, and DeAngelo, Terri, *Web Site Usability: A Designer's Guide*, Morgan Kaufmann Publishers, San Francisco, CA (1999), 156 pages.

Van Duyne, Douglas K., Landay, James A., and Hong, Jason I., *The Design of Sites: Patterns, Principles, and Processes for Crafting a Customer-Centered Web Experience*, Addison-Wesley, Reading, MA (2002), 816 pages.

Collections

Classic collections

Adler, Paul S. and Winograd, Terry (Editors), *Usability: Turning Technologies into Tools*, Oxford University Press, New York (1992), 208 pages.

Badre, Albert and Shneiderman, Ben (Editors), *Directions in Human-Computer Interaction*, Ablex, Norwood, NJ (1980), 225 pages.

Carey, Jane (Editor), *Human Factors in Management Information Systems*, Ablex, Norwood, NJ (1988), 289 pages.

Carroll, John M. (Editor), *Interfacing Thought: Cognitive Aspects of Human-Computer Interaction*, MIT Press, Cambridge, MA (1987), 324 pages.

Carroll, John M. (Editor), *Designing Interaction: Psychology at the Human-Computer Interface*, Cambridge University Press, Cambridge, UK (1991), 333 pages.

Durrett, H. John (Editor), *Color and the Computer*, Academic Press, San Diego, CA (1987), 299 pages.

Greenberg, Saul (Editor), *Computer-Supported Cooperative Work and Groupware*, Academic Press, London, UK (1991), 423 pages.

Hartson, H. Rex (Editor), *Advances in Human-Computer Interaction*, Volume 1, Ablex, Norwood, NJ (1985), 290 pages.

Helander, Martin (Editor), *Handbook of Human-Computer Interaction*, North-Holland, Amsterdam, The Netherlands (1988), 1167 pages.

Laurel, Brenda (Editor), *The Art of Human-Computer Interface Design*, Addison-Wesley, Reading, MA (1990), 523 pages.

Nielsen, Jakob (Editor), *Advances in Human-Computer Interaction*, Volume 5, Ablex, Norwood, NJ (1993), 258 pages.

Norman, Donald A. and Draper, Stephen W. (Editors), *User Centered System Design: New Perspectives on Human-Computer Interaction*, Lawrence Erlbaum Associates, Hillsdale, NJ (1986).

Shackel, Brian and Richardson, Simon (Editors), *Human Factors for Informatics Usability*, Cambridge University Press, Cambridge, UK (1991), 438 pages.

Shneiderman, Ben (Editor), *Sparks of Innovation in Human-Computer Interaction*, Ablex, Norwood, NJ (1993), 387 pages.

Thomas, John C. and Schneider, Michael L. (Editors), *Human Factors in Computer Systems*, Ablex, Norwood, NJ (1984), 276 pages.

Van Cott, H. P. and Kinkade, R. G. (Editors), *Human Engineering Guide to Equipment Design*, U.S. Superintendent of Documents, Washington, DC (1972), 752 pages.

Wiener, Earl L., and Nagel, David C. (Editors), *Human Factors in Aviation*, Academic Press, New York (1988), 684 pages.

Recent collections

Baecker, R., Grudin, J., Buxton, W., and Greenberg, S. (Editors), *Readings in Human-Computer Interaction: Towards the Year 2000*, Morgan Kaufmann, San Francisco, CA (1995), 950 pages.

Bergman, Eric, *Information Appliances and Beyond*, Morgan Kaufmann Publishers, San Francisco, CA (2000), 384 pages.

Bias, Randolph and Mayhew, Deborah (Editors), *Cost-Justifying Usability*, Academic Press, New York (1994).

Carey, Jane (Editor), *Human Factors in Information Systems: Emerging Theoretical Bases*, Ablex, Norwood, NJ (1995), 381 pages.

Carroll, John M. (Editor), *Minimalism Beyond the NurnBerg Funnel*, MIT Press, Cambridge, MA (1998), 350 pages.

Carroll, John M. (Editor), *Human-Computer Interaction in the New Millennium*, Addison-Wesley, Reading, MA (2002), 752 pages.

Cassell, Justine and Jenkins, Henry (Editors), *From Barbie to Mortal Kombat*, MIT Press, Cambridge, MA (1998), 360 pages.

Druin, Allison (Editor), *The Design of Children's Software: How We Design, What We Design and Why*, Morgan Kaufmann Publishers, San Francisco, CA (1999).

Earnshaw, Rae, Guedj, Richard, van Dam, Andries, and Vince, John (Editors), *Frontiers in Human-Centred Computing, Online Communities and Virtual Environments*, Springer-Verlag, London, UK (2001), 504 pages.

Gardner-Bonneau, Daryle (Editor), *Human Factors and Voice Interactive Systems*, Kluwer Academic Publishers, Boston, MA (1999), 336 pages.

Greenberg, Saul, Hayne, Stephen, and Rada, Roy (Editors), *Groupware for Real Time Drawing: A Designer's Guide*, McGraw-Hill, New York (1995).

Helander, Martin, Landauer, Thomas K., and Prabhu, Prasad V. (Editors), *Handbook of Human-Computer Interaction*, North-Holland Elsevier Science, Amsterdam, The Netherlands (1997), 1582 pages.

Jacko, Julie and Sears, Andrew (Editors), *Handbook of Human-Computer Interaction*, Lawrence Erlbaum Associates, Hillsdale, NJ (2003).

MacDonald, Lindsay and Vince, John (Editors), *Interacting with Virtual Environments*, John Wiley & Sons, New York (1994), 291 pages.

Perlman, Gary, Green, Georgia K., and Wogalter, Michael S. (Editors), *Human Factors Perspectives on Human-Computer Interaction: Selections from Proceedings of Human Factors and Ergonomics Society Annual Meetings 1983–1994*, HFES, Santa Monica, CA (1995), 381 pages.

Rudisill, Marianne, Lewis, Clayton, Polson, Peter B., and McKay, Timothy D. (Editors), *Human-Computer Interface Design: Success Stories, Emerging Methods and Real-World Context*, Morgan Kaufmann Publishers, San Francisco, CA (1995), 408 pages.

Salvendy, Gavriel (Editor), *Handbook of Human Factors: Second Edition*, John Wiley & Sons, New York (1997), 2100 pages.

Stephanidis, Constantine (Editor), *User Interfaces for All: Concepts, Methods, and Tools*, Lawrence Erlbaum Associates, Hillsdale, NJ (2001), 728 pages.

Trenner, Lesley and Bawa, Joanna (Editors), *The Politics of Usability: A Practical Guide to Designing Usable System in Industry*, Springer-Verlag, Berlin, Germany (1998), 204 pages.

Winograd, Terry (Editor), *Bringing Design to Software*, ACM Press, New York, and Addison-Wesley, Reading, MA (1996), 321 pages.

Videotapes

Video is an effective medium for presenting the dynamic, graphical, interactive nature of modern user interfaces.

The Technical Video Program of the ACM SIGCHI conferences makes it possible to see excellent demonstrations of often-cited but seldom-seen systems. All CHI videos can be ordered directly through ACM at http://www.acm.org/sigchi/video/.

"User-Interface Strategies" from the University of Maryland, Instructional Television are satellite television programs (1988–1997) with key HCI personalities. See http://www.glue.umd.edu/itv.

chapter

Theories, Principles, and Guidelines

We want principles, not only developed—the work of the closet—but applied, which is the work of life.

HORACE MANN,
Thoughts, 1867

There never comes a point where a theory can be said to be true. The most that anyone can claim for any theory is that it has shared the successes of all its rivals and that it has passed at least one test which they have failed.

A. J. AYER,
Philosophy in the Twentieth Century, 1982

Page Proofs
Non-Finalized Files

2.1 Introduction

Successful designers of interactive systems know that they can and must go beyond intuitive judgments made hastily when a design problem emerges. Fortunately, guidance for designers is available in the form of (1) high-level theories and models, (2) middle-level principles, and (3) specific and practical guidelines. For some high-level theories and models, the goal is to describe objects and actions with consistent terminology so that comprehensible explanations can be made to support communication and teaching. Other theories are predictive, such as those for reading, typing, or pointing times. The middle-level principles help in analyzing and comparing design alternatives. The practical guidelines prescribe cures for design problems, caution against dangers, and provide helpful reminders based on accumulated wisdom.

In many contemporary systems, there is a grand opportunity to improve the user interface. The cluttered displays, complex and tedious procedures, inadequate functionality, inconsistent sequences of actions, and insufficient informative feedback can generate debilitating stress and anxiety. These can lead to poor performance, frequent minor slips, and occasional serious errors, all contributing to job dissatisfaction and consumer frustration. Theories, principles, and guidelines can provide remedies for these problems.

This chapter begins with a review of several theories, concentrating on the object-action interface model in Section 2.3. Section 2.4 then deals with frequency of use, task profiles, and interaction styles. Eight golden rules of interface design are offered in Section 2.5. Strategies for preventing errors are described in Section 2.6. Specific guidelines for data display and entry appear in Sections 2.7 and 2.8. Section 2.9 addresses the difficult question of balancing automation and human control.

Theories, principles, and guidelines have matured in recent years. Reliable methods for predicting pointing and input times (Chapter 9), better frameworks for online help (Chapter 12), and helpful social theories (Chapter 14) now shape research and guide design.

2.2 High-Level Theories

Many theories are needed to describe the multiple aspects of interactive systems. Some theories are descriptive and explanatory: These qualitative theories are helpful in developing consistent terminology for objects and actions, thereby supporting collaboration and training. Some theories are predictive: They enable designers to quantitatively compare proposed designs for execution time or error rates. Prescriptive theories offer guidelines, recommend best practices, and caution about dangers—that is, they prescribe practice.

Some theories may focus on perceptual tasks (finding an item on a display) or cognitive aspects (planning the conversion of a boldfaced character to an italic one), whereas others concentrate on motor-task performance (time to point with a mouse). Motor-task predictions are well established and accurate for predicting keystroking or pointing times (see Fitts's Law, Section 9.3.5). Perceptual theories have been successful in predicting reading times for free text, lists, and formatted displays. However, predicting performance on complex cognitive tasks (combinations of subtasks) is especially difficult because of the many strategies that might be employed and the many opportunities for going astray. The ratio for times to perform complex tasks between novices and experts or between first-time and frequent users can be as high as 100 to 1. Actually, the contrast is even more dramatic, because novices and first-time users often are unable to complete the tasks.

A *taxonomy* is a part of a descriptive or explanatory theory. A taxonomy is the result of someone trying to impose order on a complex set of phenomena; for example, a taxonomy might be created for different kinds of input devices (direct versus indirect, linear versus rotary, 1-, 2-, 3- or higher dimensional) (Card *et al.*, 1990). Other taxonomies might cover tasks (structured versus unstructured, controllable versus immutable) (Norman, 1991), personality styles (convergent versus divergent, field dependent versus independent), technical aptitudes (spatial visualization, reasoning) (Egan, 1988), user experience levels (novice, knowledgeable, expert), or user-interface styles (menus, form fill-in, commands). Taxonomies facilitate useful comparisons, organize topics for newcomers, guide designers, and often indicate opportunities for novel products.

Any theory that might help designers to predict performance for even a limited range of users, tasks, or designs is a contribution (Card, 1989). At the moment, the field is filled with hundreds of theories competing for attention while being refined by their promoters, extended by critics, and applied by eager and hopeful—but skeptical—designers. This development is healthy for the emerging discipline of human-computer interaction, but it means that practitioners must keep up with the rapid developments not only in software tools but also in theories.

Another direction for theoreticians would be to try to predict subjective satisfaction or emotional reactions of users. Researchers in media and advertising have recognized the difficulty in predicting emotional reactions, so they complement theoretical predictions with their intuitive judgments and extensive market testing. Broader theories of small-group behavior, organizational dynamics, sociology of knowledge, and technology adoption may prove to be useful. Similarly, the methods of anthropology or social psychology may be helpful in understanding and overcoming barriers to new technology and resistance to change.

There may be "nothing so practical as a good theory," but coming up with an effective theory is often difficult. By definition, a theory, taxonomy, or model is an abstraction of reality and therefore must be incomplete. However, a good theory should at least be understandable, produce similar conclusions for all who use it, and help to solve specific practical problems.

2.2.1 Conceptual, semantic, syntactic, and lexical model

An appealing and easily comprehensible descriptive model is the four-level approach that Foley and van Dam developed in the late 1970s (Foley *et al.*, 1990):

1. The *conceptual level* is the user's mental model of the interactive system. Two conceptual models for image creation are paint programs that manipulate pixels and drawing programs that operate on objects.

2. The *semantic level* describes the meanings conveyed by the user's input and by the computer's output display. For example, deleting an object could be accomplished by undoing an operation or by applying an eraser.
3. The *syntactic level* defines how the units (words) that convey semantics are assembled into a complete sentence that instructs the computer to perform a certain task. For example, "undo" could be invoked by an operation or a gesture.
4. The *lexical level* deals with device dependencies and with the precise mechanisms by which a user specifies the syntax (e.g., a function key or a mouse click).

This approach is convenient for designers because its top-down nature is easy to explain, matches the software architecture, and allows for useful modularity during design. Designers are expected to move from conceptual to lexical and to record carefully the mappings between levels. This model was very effective in the early days of computing, when command-line input was common and implementers had to write low-level syntax and lexical-analysis programs. Since modern graphical user interface standards and toolkits have greatly reduced the need to design or implement syntactic and lexical levels, this model is less relevant today.

2.2.2 GOMS and the keystroke-level model

Card, Moran, and Newell (1980, 1983) proposed the *goals, operators, methods, and selection rules* (GOMS) model and the *keystroke-level model.* They postulated that users formulate goals (edit document) and subgoals (insert word), each of which they achieve by using methods or procedures (move cursor to desired location by following a sequence of arrow keys). The operators are "elementary perceptual, motor, or cognitive acts, whose execution is necessary to change any aspect of the user's mental state or to affect the task environment" (Card *et al.*, 1983, p. 144) (press up-arrow key, move hand to mouse, recall file name, verify that cursor is at end of file). The selection rules are the control structures for choosing among the several methods available for accomplishing a goal (delete by repeated backspace versus delete by placing markers at beginning and end of region and pressing Delete button).

The keystroke-level model attempts to explain cognitive processes and predict performance times for error-free expert performance of tasks by summing up the times for keystroking, pointing, homing, drawing, thinking, and waiting for the system to respond. Card, Moran, and Newell describe an idealized model human processor whose activity describes the essential features of user behavior. Critics complained that GOMS concentrates on expert users and error-free performance and places insufficient emphasis on learning, problem solving, error handling, subjective satisfaction, and retention.

Kieras and Polson (1985) built on the GOMS approach and used production rules to describe the conditions and actions in an interactive text editor. The number and complexity of production rules gave accurate predictions of learning and performance times for five text-editing operations: insert, delete, copy, move, and transpose. Other strategies for modeling interactive-system usage involve *transition diagrams* (Fig. 2.1). These diagrams are helpful during design, for instruction, and as a predictor of learning time, performance time, and errors.

Kieras (1988), however, complains that the Card, Moran, and Newell presentation "does not explain in any detail how the notation works, and it seems somewhat clumsy to use. Furthermore, the notation has only a weak connection to the underlying cognitive theory." Kieras offers a refinement, with his *Natural GOMS Language* (NGOMSL), and an analysis method for writing down GOMS models. He tries to clarify the situations in which the

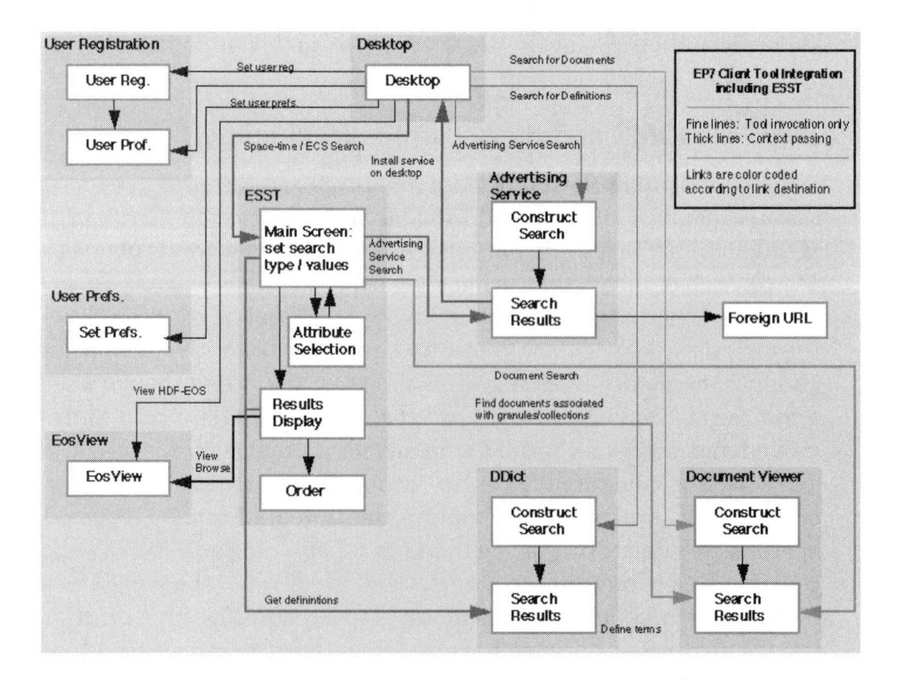

Figure 2.1

Transition diagram from the NASA search system.

GOMS task analyst must make a *judgment call,* must make assumptions about how users view the system, must bypass a complex hard-to-analyze task (choosing wording of a sentence, finding a bug in a program), or must check for consistency. Applying NGOMSL to guide the process of creating online help, Elkerton and Palmiter (1991) developed *method descriptions* for their interface, in which the actions necessary to accomplish a goal are broken down into steps. They also developed *selection rules,* by which a user can choose among alternative methods. For example, there may be two alternative methods to delete fields and one selection rule:

- Method 1 to accomplish the goal of deleting the field:

Step 1:	Decide: If necessary, then accomplish the goal of selecting the field.
Step 2:	Accomplish the goal of using a specific field-delete method.
Step 3:	Report goal accomplished.

- Method 2 to accomplish the goal of deleting the field:

Step 1:	Decide: If necessary, then use the Browse tool to go to the card with the field.
Step 2:	Choose the Field tool in the Tools menu.
Step 3:	Note that the fields on the card background are displayed.
Step 4:	Click on the field to be selected.
Step 5:	Report goal accomplished.

- Selection rule set for goal of using a specific field-delete method:
  - If you want to paste the field somewhere else, then choose "Cut Field" from the Edit menu.
  - If you want to delete the field permanently, then choose "Clear Field" from the Edit menu.
- Report goal accomplished.

The empirical evaluation with 28 subjects demonstrated that the NGOMSL version of help halved the time users took to complete information searches in the first of four trial blocks.

A production-rule–based cognitive architecture called Soar provides a computer-based approach to implementing GOMS models. This software tool enables complex predictions of expert performance times based on perceptual and cognitive parameters—for example, Soar was used to model learning in the highly interactive task of video-game playing (Bauer and John, 1995). John and Kieras (1996a, 1996b) compare four GOMS-related techniques and provide 10 case studies of practical applications.

2.2.3 Stages of action models

Another approach to forming theories is to portray the stages of action that users go through in trying to use interactive products such as information appliances, office tools, and Web interfaces. Norman (1988) offers seven stages of action as an explanatory model of human-computer interaction:

1. Forming the goal
2. Forming the intention
3. Specifying the action
4. Executing the action
5. Perceiving the system state
6. Interpreting the system state
7. Evaluating the outcome

Some of Norman's stages correspond roughly to Foley and van Dam's separation of concerns; that is, the user forms a conceptual intention, reformulates it into the semantics of several commands, constructs the required syntax, and eventually produces the lexical token by the action of moving the mouse to select a point on the screen. Norman makes a contribution by placing his stages in the context of *cycles of action* and *evaluation*. This dynamic process of action distinguishes Norman's approach from the other models, which deal mainly with the knowledge that must be in the user's mind. Furthermore, the seven-stages model leads naturally to identification of the *gulf of execution* (the mismatch between the user's intentions and the allowable actions) and the *gulf of evaluation* (the mismatch between the system's representation and the user's expectations).

This model leads Norman to suggest four principles of good design. First, the state and the action alternatives should be visible. Second, there should be a good conceptual model with a consistent system image. Third, the interface should include good mappings that reveal the relationships between stages. Fourth, users should receive continuous feedback. Norman places a heavy emphasis on studying errors, describing how errors often occur in moving from goals to intentions to actions and to executions.

A stages-of-action model helps us to describe user exploration of an interface (Polson and Lewis, 1990). As users try to accomplish their goals, there are four critical points where user failures can occur: (1) users can form an inadequate goal, (2) users might not find the correct interface object because of an incomprehensible label or icon, (3) users many not know how to specify or execute a desired action, and (4) users may receive inappropriate or misleading feedback. The latter three failures may be prevented by improved design or overcome by time-consuming experience with the interface (Franzke, 1995).

2.2.4 Consistency through grammars

An important goal for designers is a *consistent* user interface. However, the definition of consistency is elusive and has multiple levels that are sometimes in conflict; it is also sometimes advantageous to be inconsistent. The argument for consistency is that a command language or set of actions should be orderly, predictable, describable by a few rules, and therefore easy to learn and retain. These overlapping concepts are conveyed by an example that shows two kinds of inconsistency (A illustrates lack of any attempt at consistency, and B shows consistency except for a single violation):

CONSISTENT	INCONSISTENT A	INCONSISTENT B
delete/insert character	delete/insert character	delete/insert character
delete/insert word	remove/bring word	remove/insert word
delete/insert line	destroy/create line	delete/insert line
delete/insert paragraph	kill/birth paragraph	delete/insert paragraph

Each of the actions in the consistent version is the same, whereas the actions vary for the inconsistent version A. The inconsistent action verbs are all acceptable, but their variety suggests that they will take longer to learn, will cause more errors, will slow down users, and will be harder for users to remember. Inconsistent version B is somehow more malicious, because there is a single unpredictable inconsistency that stands out so dramatically that this language is likely to be remembered for its peculiar inconsistency.

To capture these notions, Reisner (1981) proposed an *action grammar* to describe two versions of a graphics-system interface. She demonstrated that the version that had a simpler grammar was easier to learn. Payne and Green (1986) expanded her work by addressing the multiple levels of consistency (lexical, syntactic, and semantic) through a notational structure they call *task-action grammars* (TAGs). They also address some aspects of completeness of a language by trying to characterize a complete set of tasks; for example, *up*, *down*, and *left* constitute an incomplete set of arrow-cursor movement tasks, because *right* is missing. Once the full set of task-action mappings is written down, the grammar of the command language can be tested against it to demonstrate completeness. Of course, a designer might leave out something from the task-action mapping, such that the grammar could not be checked accurately, but it still seems useful to have an approach to checking for completeness and consistency. For example, a TAG definition of cursor control would have a dictionary of tasks:

move-cursor-one-character-forward	[Direction = forward, Unit = char]
move-cursor-one-character-backward	[Direction = backward, Unit = char]
move-cursor-one-word-forward	[Direction = forward, Unit = word]
move-cursor-one-word-backward	[Direction = backward, Unit = word]

The high-level rule schemas that describe the syntax of the commands would be as follows:

1. task [Direction, Unit] → symbol [Direction] + letter [Unit]
2. symbol [Direction = forward] → "CTRL"
3. symbol [Direction = backward] → "ESC"
4. letter [Unit = word] → "W"
5. letter [Unit = char] → "C"

These schemas will generate a consistent grammar:

move cursor one character forward	CTRL-C
move cursor one character backward	ESC-C
move cursor one word forward	CTRL-W
move cursor one word backward	ESC-W

Payne and Green are careful to state that their notation and approach are flexible and extensible, and they provide appealing examples in which using their approach sharpened the thinking of designers.

Reisner (1990) extends this work by defining consistency more formally, but Grudin (1989) points out flaws in some arguments for consistency. Certainly consistency is subtle and has multiple levels; however, there are conflicting forms of consistency, and sometimes inconsistency is a virtue (for example, to draw attention to a dangerous operation). Nonetheless, understanding consistency is an important goal for designers and researchers.

2.2.5 Widget-level theories

Hierarchical decomposition is often a useful tool for dealing with complexity, but many of the theories and predictive models follow an extreme reductionist approach, which may not always be valid. In some situations, it is hard to accept the low level of detail, the precise numbers that are sometimes attached to subtasks, and the validity of simple summations of time periods. Furthermore, models requiring numerous subjective judgments raise the question of whether several analysts would come up with the same results.

An alternative approach is to follow the simplifications made in the higher-level user-interface–building tools (see Chapter 5). Instead of dealing with atomic-level features, why not create a model based on the widgets (interface components) supported in the tool? Once a scrolling-list widget was tested to determine user performance as a function of the number of items and the size of the window, the performance of future widget users could be predicted automatically. The prediction would have to be derived from some declaration of the task frequencies, but the description of the interface would emerge from the process of designing the interface. A measure of layout appropriateness (frequently used pairs of widgets should be adjacent, and the left-to-right sequence should be in harmony with the task-sequence description) would also be produced to guide the designer in a possible redesign. Estimates of the perceptual and cognitive complexity plus the motor load would be generated automatically (Sears, 1992).

As widgets become more sophisticated and more widely used, the investment in determining the complexity of each widget will be amortized over the many designers and projects.

Gradually, richer patterns of usage are appearing, in much the way that Alexander describes has occurred in architecture (1977). Familiar patterns of building fireplaces, stairways, or roofs become modular components that acquire names and are combined to form still larger patterns. Patterns are an alternative to guidelines, with the distinguishing feature that patterns promise an orderly structure of problem, context, solution, examples, and cross referencing. Patterns for human-computer interaction—such as "multiple ways to navigate," "process funnel," and "internationalized and localized content"—have been identified for desktop applications, mobile devices, and Web design (Van Duyne, Landay, and Hong, 2002).

2.2.6 Situated action and distributed cognition

While the reductionist methods of experimental and cognitive psychology were a profound influence on early work in human-computer interaction, a growing awareness of the special needs of this new discipline led to the rise of alternative theories. The complaints against tightly controlled laboratory studies of isolated phenomena grew from researchers and practitioners. Investigators of workplace and home computing identified the critical role of complex interactions among people and with other electronic devices and paper resources. For example, successful users of interfaces often had nearby colleagues to ask for help or required diverse documents to complete their tasks. Unexpected interruptions were a regular part of life, and sticky notes attached to the sides of computers were often consulted for vital information. In short, the physical and social environments were inextricably intertwined with use of computer and information technologies. Design could not be separated from patterns of use.

Suchman's (1987) analysis in her book *Plans and Situated Action* is often credited with launching this reconsideration of human-computer interaction. She argued that the cognitive model of orderly human plans that were executed when needed was insufficient to describe the richer and livelier world of work or personal usage. She proposed that users' actions were situated in time and place, making user behavior highly responsive to other people and to environmental contingencies. If users got stuck in using an interface, they might ask for help, depending on who was around, or consult a manual (if it were available). If they were pressed for time, they might risk some shortcuts, but if the work was life-critical they would be extra cautious. Rather than having fixed plans, users were constantly changing their plans in response to the circumstances.

The argument of distributed cognition was that knowledge was not only in the users' minds, but distributed in their environments—some knowledge was stored on paper documents, maintained by computers, or available from colleagues. Proponents of distributed cognition emphasized this distinction from the model human processor described by Card, Moran, and Newell as the basis for GOMS (Scaife and Rogers, 1996).

Other alternative models of technology use emphasized the social environment, motivations of users, or the role of experience. Innovators believed that turbulence of actual usage, as opposed to idealized task specifications, meant that users had to be more than test subjects—they had to be participants in design processes (Greenbaum and Kyng, 1991). Breakdowns were often seen as the source of insight about design, encouraging users to become reflective practitioners who are continuously engaged in the process of design refinement. Understanding the transition from novice to expert and the differences in skill levels became a focus of attention, further calling into question the utility of hour-long laboratory or half-day usability-testing studies as a guide to behavior of users after a month or more of experience. These movements encouraged greater attention to detailed ethnographic observation, longitudinal case studies, and action research by participant observers (Nardi, 1997; Redmiles, 2002).

2.3 Object-Action Interface Model

Resolving the battles between those who emphasize cognitive models of user knowledge versus the lively dynamics of actual usage might be accomplished by addressing both. There are many ways to pursue this goal, so the constraint of having to support design, documentation, and training processes is helpful.

The maturing model described in this book's first edition stressed the separation between task-domain concepts (for example, stock-market portfolios) and the computer-domain concepts that represent them (for example, folders, spreadsheets, or databases). This book's second edition amplified the important distinction between objects and actions, paralleling the familiar separation between nouns and verbs. In the third edition, the underlying theory of design was called the *object-action interface* (OAI—let's pronounce it Oo-Ah!) *model*. The OAI model is descriptive and explanatory, and it can also be prescriptive, in that it provides valuable guidance for designers of interfaces, online help, and training processes.

As GUIs have replaced command languages, intricate syntax has given way to relatively simple direct manipulations applied to visual representations of objects and actions. The emphasis is now on the visual display of user-task objects and actions. For example, a collection of stock-market portfolios might be represented by leather folders with icons of engraved share certificates; likewise, actions might be represented by trash cans for deletion, or shelf icons to represent destinations for portfolio copying. Of course, there are syntactic aspects of direct manipulation, such as knowing whether to drag the file to the trash can or vice versa, but the amount of syntax is small and can be thought of as being at the lowest level of the interface actions. Even syntactic forms such as double-clicking, mouse-down-and-wait, or gestures seem simple compared to the pages of grammars for early command languages.

Doing object-action design starts with understanding the task. That task includes the universe of real-world objects with which users work to accomplish their intentions and the actions that they apply to those objects. The high-level task objects might be stock-market statistics, a photo library, or a personal phone book (Fig. 2.2). These objects can be decomposed into information on a single stock, for example, and finally into atomic units, such as a share price. Task actions start from high-level intentions that are decomposed into intermediate goals and individual steps.

To accommodate the arguments of situated action and distributed cognition, the objects may include real-world items (such as books, maps, or other devices) and the actions may include common activities (such as speaking to colleagues, handling interruptions, or answering telephones). These may be described as part of a model of user activity, but they form a separate category since designers may have little influence on them or how they are used.

Once there is agreement on the task objects and actions and their decomposition, the designer can create the metaphoric representations of the interface objects and actions. Interface objects do not have weight or thickness; they are pixels that can be moved or copied in ways that represent real-world task objects with feedback to guide users. Finally, the

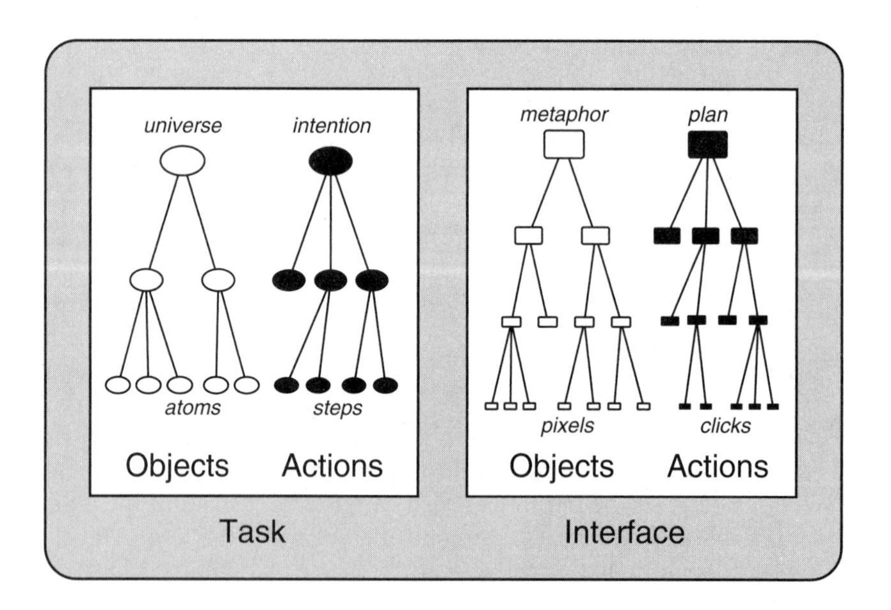

Figure 2.2

Task and interface concepts, separated into hierarchies of objects and actions.

designer must make the interface actions visible to users, so that users can decompose their plans into a series of intermediate actions, such as opening a dialog box, all the way down to a series of detailed keystrokes and clicks.

In outline, the OAI model is a descriptive and explanatory model that focuses on task and interface objects and actions. Because the syntactic details are minimal, users who know the task-domain objects and actions can learn the interface relatively easily (see Chapter 12). The OAI model also reflects the higher level of design with which most designers deal when they use the widgets in user-interface–building tools. The standard widgets have familiar and simple syntax (click, double-click, drag, or drop) and simple forms of feedback (highlighting, scrolling, or movement), leaving designers free to focus on how these widgets create a business-oriented solution. The OAI model is in harmony with popular programming methods and software-engineering trends toward object-oriented design.

2.3.1 Task hierarchies of objects and actions

The primary way people deal with large and complex problems is to decompose them into several smaller problems, in a hierarchical manner, until each subproblem is manageable. For example, a human body is discussed in terms of neural, muscular, skeletal, reproductive, digestive, circulatory, and other subsystems, which in turn might be described by organs, tissues, and cells. Most real-world objects have similar decompositions: buildings, cities, computer programs, human genomes, and plays, for example. Some objects are more neatly decomposable than others, and some objects are easier to understand than others.

A symphony performance has movements, measures, and notes; a baseball game has innings, outs, and pitches. Similarly, intentions can be decomposed into smaller action steps. A building-construction plan can be reduced to a series of steps, such as surveying the property, laying the foundation, building the frame, raising the roof, and completing the interior.

People learn the task objects and actions independently of their implementation on a computer. People learn about buildings or books through developmental experiences in their youth, but many tasks require specialized training, such as in how to manage stock-market portfolios, to design buildings, or to diagnose medical problems. It may take years to learn the terminology, to acquire the decision-making skills, and to become proficient.

Designers who develop computer systems to support professionals may have to take training courses, read workbooks, and interview users.

Page Proofs
Non-Finalized Files

Then, the designers can sit down and generate a hierarchy of objects and actions to model the users' tasks. This model forms a basis for designing the interface objects and actions plus their representation in pixels on a screen, in physical devices, or by a voice or other audio cue.

Users who must learn to use computers to accomplish real-world tasks must first become proficient in the task domain. An expert computer user who has not studied architecture will not be able to effectively use a building-design package any more than a computer-savvy amateur can make reliable medical diagnoses.

In summary, tasks include hierarchies of objects and actions at high and low levels. Hierarchies are not perfect, but they are comprehensible and useful. Most users accept a separation of their tasks into high- and low-level objects and actions.

2.3.2 Interface hierarchies of objects and actions

Like tasks, interfaces include hierarchies of objects and actions at high and low levels. For example, a central set of *interface-object* concepts deals with storage. Users come to understand the high-level concept that computers store information. The stored information can then be refined into objects, such as a directory and the files of information it contains. In turn, the directory object is refined into a set of directory entries, each of which has a name, length, date of creation, owner, access-control setting, and so on. Likewise, each file is an object that has a lower-level structure consisting of lines, fields, characters, fonts, pointers, and so on.

The *interface actions* also are decomposable into lower-level actions. The high-level plans, such as creating a text data file, may require load, insertion, and save actions. The mid-level action of saving a file is refined into the actions of storing a file and a backup file on one of many disks, applying access-control rights, overwriting previous versions, assigning a name to the file, and so on. There are also many low-level details about permissible file types or sizes, error conditions such as shortage of storage space, or responses to hardware or software errors. Finally, users carry out the low-level action of issuing a specific command by clicking on a pull-down menu item.

Designers craft interface objects and actions based on familiar examples, then tune those objects and actions to fit the task. For example, in developing a system to manage stock-market portfolios, the designer might consider spreadsheets, databases, word processors, or a specialized graphical design that allows users to drag stock symbols to a buying or selling icon.

Users can learn about interface objects and actions by seeing a demonstration, hearing an explanation of features, or conducting trial-and-error sessions. The metaphoric representation—abstract, concrete, or analogical—conveys the interface objects and actions. For example, to explain saving a file, an instructor might draw a picture of a disk drive and a directory to show where the file goes and how the directory references the file. Alternatively, the instructor might describe how the card catalog acts as a directory for books saved in the library.

When interface objects and actions have a logical structure that can be anchored to familiar task objects and actions, we expect that structure to be relatively stable in memory. If users remember the high-level concept of saving a file, they will be able to conclude that the file must have a name, a size, and a storage location. The linkage to other objects and the visual presentation can enhance the memorability of this knowledge.

These interface objects and actions were once novel, known by only a small number of scientists, engineers, and data-processing professionals. Now, these concepts are taught at the elementary-school level, argued over during coffee breaks in the office, and exchanged in the aisles of corporate jets. When educators talk of computer literacy, part of their plans cover these interface concepts.

The OAI model helps us to understand the multiple complex processes that must occur for users to be successful in using an interface to accomplish a task. For example, in writing a business letter using computer software, users have to integrate smoothly their knowledge of the task objects and actions and of the interface objects and actions. They must have the high-level concept of writing (task action) a letter (task object), recognize that the letter will be stored as a document (interface object), and know the details of the save command (interface action). Users must be fluent with the middle-level concept of composing a sentence and must recognize the mechanisms for beginning, writing, and ending a sentence. Finally, users must know the proper low-level details of spelling each word (low-level task object), and must know where the keys are for each letter (low-level interface object). The goal of minimizing interface concepts (such as the syntax of a command language) while presenting a visual representation of the task objects and actions is the heart of the direct-manipulation approach to design (see Chapter 6).

Integrating the multiple levels of task and interface concepts is a substantial challenge that requires great motivation and concentration. Educational materials that facilitate the acquisition of this knowledge are difficult to design, especially because of the diversity of background knowledge and motivation levels of typical learners. The OAI model of user knowledge can provide a guide to educational designers by highlighting the different kinds of knowledge that users need to acquire (see Chapter 12).

Designers of interactive systems can apply the OAI model to systematize their work. Where possible, the task objects should be made explicit, and the user's task actions should be laid out clearly. Then, the interface objects and actions can be identified, and appropriate representations can be created. These designs are likely to increase comprehensibility to users and independence from specific hardware. Criteria for design quality are emerging based on the fact that small numbers of objects and actions tend to be easier to learn. Designers would do well to determine how fine a granularity of objects to use and how many different actions are needed.

2.3.3 The disappearance of syntax

In the early days of computers, users had to maintain a profusion of device-dependent details in their human memories. These low-level syntactic details included the knowledge of which action erases a character (Delete, Backspace, Ctrl-H, Ctrl-G, Ctrl-D, rightmost mouse button, or Escape), which action inserts a new line after the third line of a text file (Ctrl-I, Insert key, I3, I 3, or 3I), which abbreviations are permissible, and which of the numbered function keys produces the previous screen.

The learning, use, and retention of this knowledge are hampered by two problems. First, these details vary across systems in an unpredictable manner. Second, acquiring syntactic knowledge is often a struggle because the arbitrariness of these minor design features greatly reduces the effectiveness of paired-associate learning. Rote memorization requires repeated rehearsals to reach competence, and retention over time is poor unless the knowledge is applied frequently.

In some cases, a further problem with syntactic knowledge lies in the difficulty of providing a hierarchical structure or even a modular structure to cope with the complexity. For example, it may be hard for a user to remember these details of using an electronic-mail system: press Return to terminate a paragraph, Ctrl-D to terminate a letter, Q to quit the electronic-mail subsystem, and log out to terminate the session. The knowledgeable computer user understands these four forms of termination as commands in the context of the full system, but the novice may be confused by four seemingly similar situations that have radically inconsistent syntactic forms.

A final difficulty is that syntactic knowledge is system-dependent. A user who switches from one machine to another may face different keyboard layouts, commands, function-key usage, and sequences of actions. One system may use K to keep a file and Ctrl-S to save, while another uses K to kill the file and Ctrl-S to send.

Expert frequent users can overcome these difficulties, and they tend to be less troubled by syntactic knowledge problems. Novices and knowledgeable but intermittent users, however, are especially troubled by syntactic irregularities. Their burden can be lightened by use of menus (see Chapter 7), a reduction in the arbitrariness of the keypresses, use of consistent patterns of commands, meaningful command names and labels on keys, and fewer details that must be memorized (see Chapter 8).

Minimizing these burdens is the goal of most interface designers. Modern direct-manipulation styles (see Chapter 6) support the process of presenting users with screens filled with familiar objects and actions representing their task objects and actions. Modern user-interface–building tools (see Chapter 5) facilitate the design process by making standard widgets easily available. Innovative designers may recognize opportunities for novel widgets that provide a closer match between the screen representation and the user's workplace.

2.4 Principle 1: Recognize User Diversity

When human diversity (see Section 1.5) is multiplied by the wide range of situations, tasks, and frequencies of use, the set of design possibilities becomes enormous. The designer can respond by choosing from a spectrum of interaction styles.

A preschooler playing a graphic computer game is a long way from a reference librarian doing bibliographic searches for anxious and hurried patrons. Similarly, a professional programmer using a new operating system is a long way from a highly trained and experienced air-traffic controller. Finally, a student surfing the Net for love poems is a long way from a hotel-reservations clerk serving customers for many hours per day.

These sketches highlight the differences in users' background knowledge, training in the use of the system, frequency of use, and goals, as well as in the impact of a user error. Since no single design could satisfy all these users and situations, successful designers characterize the users and the situations as precisely and completely as possible.

2.4.1 Usage profiles

"Know thy user" was the first principle in Hansen's (1971) classic list of user-engineering principles. It is a simple idea, but a difficult and, unfortunately, often-undervalued goal. No one would argue against this principle, but many designers assume that they understand the users and users' tasks. Successful designers are aware that other people learn, think, and solve problems in different ways. Some users really do prefer to deal with tables rather than with graphs, with words instead of numbers, or with a rigid structure rather than an open-ended form.

All design should begin with an understanding of the intended users, including population profiles that reflect age, gender, physical abilities, education, cultural or ethnic background, training, motivation, goals, and personality. There are often several communities of users for a system, especially for Web applications, so the design effort is multiplied. Typical user communities—such as high-school teachers, nurses, doctors, computer programmers, museum patrons, or librarians—can be expected to have various combinations of knowledge and usage patterns. Users from different countries may each deserve special attention, and regional differences may even exist within countries. Other variables that characterize users include location (for example, urban versus rural), economic profile, disabilities, and attitudes toward using technology. Users with poor reading skills, limited education, and low motivation require special attention.

In addition to these profiles, users might be tested for such skills as comprehension of Boolean expressions, knowledge of set theory, fluency in a foreign language, or skills in human relationships. Other tests might cover such task-specific abilities as knowledge of airport city codes, stockbrokerage terminology, insurance-claims concepts, or map icons.

The process of getting to know the users is never-ending because there is so much to know and because the users keep changing. Every step in understanding the users and in recognizing them as individuals with outlooks different from the designer's own is likely to be a step closer to a successful design.

For example, a generic separation into novice or first-time, knowledgeable intermittent, and expert frequent users might lead to these differing design goals:

- *Novice or first-time users.* True novice users are assumed to know little of the task or interface concepts. By contrast, first-time users are professionals who know the task concepts but have shallow knowledge of the interface concepts. Both groups of users may arrive with learning-inhibiting anxiety about using computers. Overcoming these limitations, via instructions, dialog boxes, and online help, is a serious challenge to the designer of the interface. Restricting vocabulary to a small number of familiar, consistently used concept terms is essential to begin developing the user's knowledge. The number of actions should also be small, so that novice and first-time users can carry out simple tasks successfully and thus reduce anxiety, build confidence, and gain positive reinforcement. Informative feedback about the accomplishment of each task is helpful, and constructive, specific error messages should be provided when users make mistakes. Carefully designed paper manuals and step-by-step online tutorials may be effective.

- *Knowledgeable intermittent users.* Many people are knowledgeable but intermittent users of a variety of systems. They have stable task concepts and broad knowledge of interface concepts, but they may have difficulty retaining the structure of menus or the location of features. The burden on their memories will be lightened by orderly structure in the menus, consistent terminology, and high interface apparency, which emphasizes recognition rather than recall. Consistent sequences of actions, meaningful messages, and guides to frequent patterns of usage will help knowledgeable intermittent users to rediscover how to perform their tasks properly. Protection from danger is necessary to support relaxed exploration of features or attempts to invoke partially forgotten action sequences. These users will benefit from online help screens to fill in missing pieces of task or interface knowledge. Well-organized reference manuals are also useful.
- *Expert frequent users.* Expert "power" users are thoroughly familiar with the task and interface concepts and seek to get their work done quickly. They demand rapid response times, brief and nondistracting feedback, and the shortcuts to carry out actions with just a few keystrokes or selections. When a sequence of three or four commands is performed regularly, the frequent user is eager to create a macro or other abbreviated form to reduce the number of steps. Strings of commands, shortcuts through menus, abbreviations, and other accelerators are requirements.

These characteristics of these three classes of usage must be refined for each environment. Designing for one class is easy; designing for several is much more difficult.

When multiple usage classes must be accommodated in one system, the basic strategy is to permit a *multi-layer* (sometimes called *level-structured* or *spiral*) approach to learning. Novices can be taught a minimal subset of objects and actions with which to get started. They are most likely to make correct choices when they have only a few options and are protected from making mistakes—i.e., when they are given a *training-wheels* interface. After gaining confidence from hands-on experience, these users can choose to progress to ever-greater levels of task concepts and the accompanying interface concepts. The learning plan should be governed by the users' progress through the task concepts, with new interface concepts being chosen when they are needed to support a more complex task. For users with strong knowledge of the task and interface concepts, rapid progress is possible.

For example, novice users of a cell phone might be taught how to make/receive calls first, followed by storing numbers for frequent callees. Their progress is governed by the task domain, rather than by an alphabetical list of commands that are difficult to relate to the tasks. The multi-layer approach must be carried out in the design of not only the software, but also the user manuals, help screens, error messages, and tutorials (McGrenere, Baecker, and Booth, 2002). Multi-layer designs seem to be the most promising approach to promoting universal usability.

Another component of accommodating different usage classes is to permit user control of the density of informative feedback that the system provides. Novices want more informative feedback to confirm their actions, whereas frequent users want less distracting feedback. Similarly, it seems that frequent users like displays to be more densely packed than do novices. Finally, the pace of interaction may be varied from slow for novices to fast for frequent users.

2.4.2 Task profiles and user-needs assessment

After carefully drawing the user profile, the developers must identify the tasks. Task analysis has a long, mixed history (Bailey, 1996; Hackos and Redish, 1998). Every designer would agree that the set of tasks must be determined before design can proceed, but too often the task analysis is done informally or implicitly. If implementers find that another command can be added, the designer is often tempted to include that command in the hope that some users will find it helpful. The Palm Pilot designers were dramatically successful because they ruthlessly limited functionality (calendar, contacts, to-do list, and notes) to guarantee simplicity.

High-level task actions can be decomposed into multiple middle-level task actions, which can be further refined into atomic actions that the user executes with a single command, menu selection, and so on. Choosing the most appropriate set of atomic actions is a difficult task. If the atomic actions are too small, the users will become frustrated by the large number of actions necessary to accomplish a higher-level task. If the atomic actions are too large and elaborate, the users will need many such actions with special options, or they will not be able to get exactly what they want from the system.

The relative task frequencies are important in shaping, for example, a set of commands or a menu tree. Frequently performed tasks should be simple and quick to carry out, even at the expense of lengthening some infrequent tasks. Relative frequency of use is one of the bases for making architectural design decisions. For example, in a word processor:

- Frequent actions might be performed by special keys, such as the four cursor arrows, Insert, and Delete.
- Intermediately frequent actions might be performed by a single letter plus the Ctrl key, or by a selection from a pull-down menu—examples include underscore, center, indent, subscript, or superscript.
- Infrequent actions or complex actions might require going through a sequence of menu selections or form fill-ins—for example, to change the printing format or to revise network-protocol parameters.

A matrix of users and tasks can help designers sort out these issues (Fig. 2.3). In each box, the designer can put a check mark to indicate that

FREQUENCY OF TASK BY JOB TITLE

Task *Job title*	*Query by Patient*	*Update Data*	*Query across Patients*	*Add Relations*	*Evaluate System*
Nurse	0.14	0.11			
Physician	0.06	0.04			
Supervisor	0.01	0.01	0.04		
Appointment personnel	0.26				
Medical-record maintainer	0.07	0.04	0.04	0.01	
Clinical researcher			0.08		
Database programmer			0.02	0.02	0.05

Figure 2.3

Hypothetical frequency-of-use data for a medical clinic information system. Answering queries from appointments personnel about individual patients is the highest-frequency task.

this user carries out this task. A more precise analysis would include frequencies instead of just simple check marks. Such user-needs assessment clarifies what tasks are essential for the design and which ones could be left out to preserve system simplicity and ease of learning.

2.4.3 Interaction styles

When the task analysis is complete and the task objects and actions have been identified, the designer can choose from these primary interaction styles: menu selection, form fill-in, command language, natural language, and direct manipulation (Box 2.1). Chapters 6 through 8 explore these styles in detail; this summary gives a brief comparative overview.

Direct manipulation When a clever designer can create a visual representation of the world of action, the users' tasks can be greatly simplified, because direct manipulation of familiar objects is possible. Examples of such systems include the desktop metaphor, computer-assisted design tools, air-traffic–control systems, and games. By pointing at visual representations of objects and actions, users can carry out tasks rapidly and can observe the results immediately. Keyboard entry of commands or menu choices is replaced by use of pointing devices to select from a visible set of objects and actions. Direct manipulation is appealing to novices, is easy to remember for intermittent users, and, with careful design, can be rapid for frequent users. Chapter 6 describes direct manipulation and its application.

Menu selection In menu-selection systems, users read a list of items, select the one most appropriate to their task, and observe the effect. If the terminology and meaning of the items are understandable and distinct, users can accomplish their tasks with little learning or memorization and just a few actions. The greatest benefit may be that there is a clear structure to decision making, since all possible choices are presented at one time. This interaction style is appropriate for novice and intermittent users and can be appealing to frequent users if the display and selection mechanisms are rapid. For designers, menu-selection systems require careful task analysis to ensure that all functions are supported conveniently and that terminology is chosen carefully and used consistently. Advanced user-interface–building tools to support menu selection provide an enormous benefit by ensuring consistent screen design, validating completeness, and supporting maintenance.

Form fill-in When data entry is required, menu selection usually becomes cumbersome, and form fill-in (also called fill in the blanks) is appropriate. Users see a display of related fields, move a cursor among the fields, and enter data where desired. With the form-fill-in interaction style, users must understand the field labels, know the permissible values and the data-entry method, and be capable of responding to error messages. Since knowledge of the keyboard, labels, and permissible fields is required, some training may be necessary. This interaction style is most appropriate for knowledgeable intermittent users or frequent users. Chapter 7 provides a thorough treatment of menus and form fill-in.

Command language For frequent users, command languages provide a strong feeling of locus of control and initiative. Users learn the syntax and can often express complex possibilities rapidly, without having to read distracting prompts. However, error rates are typically high, training is necessary, and retention may be poor. Error messages and online assistance are hard to provide because of the diversity of possibilities, plus the complexity of mapping from tasks to interface concepts and syntax. Command languages and lengthier query or programming languages are the domain of expert frequent users, who often derive great satisfaction from mastering a complex set of semantics and syntax. Powerful advantages include easy history keeping and simple macro creation.

Natural language The hope that computers will respond properly to arbitrary natural-language sentences or phrases engages many researchers and system developers, in spite of limited success thus far. Natural-language interaction usually provides little context for issuing the next command, frequently requires clarification dialog, and may be slower and more cumbersome than the alternatives. Still, where users are knowledgeable about a task domain whose scope is limited and where intermittent use inhibits command-language training, there exist opportunities for natural-language interfaces (discussed at the end of Chapter 8).

Blending several interaction styles may be appropriate when the required tasks and users are diverse. For example, commands can lead the user to a form fill-in where data entry is required, or menus can be used to control a direct-manipulation environment when a suitable visualization of actions cannot be found.

Box 2.1

Advantages and disadvantages of the five primary interaction styles.

Advantages	Disadvantages
Direct manipulation	
Visually presents task concepts	May be hard to program
Allows easy learning	May require graphics display and pointing devices
Allows easy retention	
Allows errors to be avoided	
Encourages exploration	
Affords high subjective satisfaction	
Menu selection	
Shortens learning	Presents danger of many menus
Reduces keystrokes	May slow frequent users
Structures decision making	Consumes screen space
Permits use of dialog-management tools	Requires rapid display rate
Allows easy support of error handling	
Form fill-in	
Simplifies data entry	Consumes screen space
Requires modest training	
Gives convenient assistance	
Permits use of form-management tools	
Command language	
Is flexible	Has poor error handling
Appeals to "power" users	Requires substantial training and memorization
Supports user initiative	
Allows convenient creation of user-defined macros	
Natural language	
Relieves burden of learning syntax	Requires clarification dialog
	May require more keystrokes
	May not show context
	Is unpredictable

2.5 Principle 2: Use the Eight Golden Rules of Interface Design

Later chapters offer constructive guidance for using the various interaction styles presented in the previous section. This section presents underlying principles of design that are applicable in most interactive systems. These underlying principles of interface design, derived heuristically from experience, should be validated and refined by the next generation of researchers.

1. *Strive for consistency*. This rule is the most frequently violated one, but following it can be tricky because there are many forms of consistency. Consistent sequences of actions should be required in similar situations; identical terminology should be used in prompts, menus, and help screens; and consistent color, layout, capitalization, fonts, and so on should be employed throughout. Exceptions, such as no echoing of passwords or confirmation of the delete command, should be comprehensible and limited in number.
2. *Enable frequent users to use shortcuts*. As the frequency of use increases, so do the users' desires to reduce the number of interactions and to increase the pace of interaction. Abbreviations, special keys, macro facilities, and menu shortcuts are appreciated by frequent knowledgeable users. Short response times and fast display rates are other attractions for frequent users.
3. *Offer informative feedback*. For every user action, there should be system feedback. For frequent and minor actions, the response can be modest, whereas for infrequent and major actions, the response should be more substantial. Visual presentation of the objects of interest provides a convenient environment for showing changes explicitly (see the discussion of direct manipulation in Chapter 6).
4. *Design dialogs to yield closure*. Sequences of actions should be organized into groups with a beginning, middle, and end. Informative feedback at the completion of a group of actions gives operators the satisfaction of accomplishment, a sense of relief, the signal to drop contingency plans from their minds, and a signal to prepare for the next group of actions. For example, checkout sequences for e-commerce Web sites move users toward completion of their purchases, ending with a clear confirmation page.
5. *Prevent errors*. As much as possible, design the system such that users cannot make a serious error; for example, prefer menu selection to

form fill-in and do not allow alphabetic characters in numeric entry fields. If users make an error, the system should detect the error and offer simple, constructive, and specific instructions for recovery. For example, users should not have to retype an entire name-address form if they enter an invalid zip code, but rather should be guided to repair only the faulty part. Erroneous actions should leave the system state unchanged, or the system should give instructions about restoring the state.

6. *Permit easy reversal of actions*. As much as possible, actions should be reversible. This feature relieves anxiety, since the user knows that errors can be undone, thus encouraging exploration of unfamiliar options. The units of reversibility may be a single action, a data-entry task, or a complete group of actions, such as entry of a name and address block.
7. *Support internal locus of control*. Experienced operators strongly desire the sense that they are in charge of the system and that the system responds to their actions. Surprising system actions, tedious sequences of data entries, inability to obtain or difficulty in obtaining necessary information, and inability to produce the action desired all build anxiety and dissatisfaction. Gaines (1981) captured part of this principle with his rule *avoid acausality* and his encouragement to make users the *initiators* of actions rather than the *responders* to actions.
8. *Reduce short-term memory load*. The limitation of human information processing in short-term memory (the rule of thumb is that humans can remember "seven plus or minus two chunks" of information) requires that displays be kept simple, multiple-page displays be consolidated, window-motion frequency be reduced, and sufficient training time be allotted for codes, mnemonics, and sequences of actions. Where appropriate, online access to command-syntax forms, abbreviations, codes, and other information should be provided.

These underlying principles must be interpreted, refined, and extended for each environment. They have their limitations but provide a good starting point for mobile, desktop, or Web designers. The principles presented in the ensuing sections focus on increasing the productivity of users by providing simplified data-entry procedures, comprehensible displays, and rapid informative feedback to increase feelings of competence, mastery, and control over the system.

2.6 Principle 3: Prevent Errors

There is no medicine against death, and against error no rule has been found.

—*SIGMUND FREUD*
(INSCRIPTION HE WROTE ON HIS PORTRAIT)

Users of word processors, spreadsheets, database-query facilities, air-traffic–control systems, and other interactive systems make mistakes far more frequently than might be expected. Even experienced authors make errors in almost half their spreadsheets (Brown and Gould, 1987). Other studies reveal the magnitude of the problem of—and the loss of productivity due to—user errors (Panko and Halverson, 1996).

One way to reduce the loss in productivity due to errors is to improve the error messages provided by the computer system. Shneiderman (1982) reported on five experiments in which changes to error messages led to improved success at repairing the errors, lower error rates, and increased subjective satisfaction. Superior error messages were more specific, positive in tone, and constructive (telling the user what to do, rather than merely reporting the problem). Rather than using vague and hostile messages, such as "Syntax Error" or "Illegal Data," designers were encouraged to use informative messages, such as "Unmatched Left Parentheses" or "Menu Choices Are in the Range of 1 to 6."

Improved error messages, however, are only helpful medicine. A more effective approach is to prevent the errors from occurring. This goal is more attainable than it may seem in many systems.

The first step is to understand the nature of errors. One perspective is that people make mistakes or "slips" (Norman, 1983) that designers can help them to avoid by organizing screens and menus functionally, designing commands or menu choices to be distinctive, and making it difficult for users to take irreversible actions. Norman offers other guidelines too, such as not having modes, offering feedback about the state of the system, and designing for consistency of commands. Norman's analysis provides practical examples and a useful theory.

Three techniques can help reduce errors by ensuring complete and correct actions: use correct matching pairs, complete sequences, and correct commands.

Correct matching pairs A common problem is the lack of correct matching pairs. This problem has many manifestations and several simple prevention strategies. An example is the failure to provide the right parenthesis to close an open left parenthesis. If a bibliographic-search system allowed Boolean expressions such as "Computers and (Psychology or Sociology)" and the user failed to provide the right parenthesis at the end, the system would produce a "Syntax Error" message or, more helpfully, a more meaningful message, such as "Unmatched Left Parentheses." Similarly, in HTML Web programming, marker pairs are required to delimit boldface, italic, or underscored text. If the text file contains <B>This is boldface</B>, then the three words between the markers appear in boldface. If the rightmost </B> is missing, additional text may inadvertently be made bold.

In each of these cases, a matching pair of markers is necessary for the operation to be complete and correct. The omission of the closing marker can be prevented by use of an editor that puts both the beginning and ending components of the pair on the screen in one action. For example, typing a left parenthesis generates a left and right parenthesis and puts the cursor in between to allow creation of the contents. An attempt to delete one of the parentheses will cause the matching parenthesis (and possibly the contents as well) to be deleted. Thus, the text can never be in a syntactically incorrect form. Some people find this rigid approach to be too restrictive. For them, a milder form of protection may be appropriate. For example, when the user types a left parenthesis, the screen displays in the lower-left corner a message indicating the need for a right parenthesis (until that character is typed).

Complete sequences Sometimes, an action requires several steps to reach completion. Since people may forget to complete every step of an action, designers attempt to offer a sequence of steps as a single action. In an automobile, the driver does not have to set two switches to signal a left turn. A single switch causes both (front and rear) turn-signal lights on the left side of the car to flash. When a pilot throws a switch to lower the landing gear, hundreds of steps and checks are invoked automatically. This same concept can be applied to interactive uses of computers. For example, the sequence of dialing up, setting communication parameters, logging on, and loading files is frequently executed by many users. Fortunately, most communications-software packages enable users to specify these processes once and then to execute them by simply selecting the appropriate process name.

As another example, users of a word processor should be able to indicate that section titles are to be centered, set in uppercase letters, and underlined, without having to issue a series of commands each time they enter a section title. Then, if the user wants to change the title style—for example, to eliminate underlining—a single command will guarantee that all section titles are revised consistently. As a final example, air-traffic controllers may formulate plans to change the altitude of a plane from 14,000 feet to 18,000 feet in two increments; after raising the plane to 16,000 feet, however, the controller may get distracted and may thus fail to complete the action. The controller should be able to record the plan and then have the computer prompt for completion.

The notion of complete sequences of actions may be difficult to implement because users may need to issue atomic actions as well as complete sequences. In this case, users should be allowed to define sequences of their own; the macro or subroutine concept should be available at every level of usage. Designers can gather information about potential complete sequences by studying sequences of commands that people actually issue and the patterns of errors that people actually make.

Correct commands Industrial designers recognize that successful products must be safe and must prevent the user from making dangerously incorrect use of the product. Airplane engines cannot be put into reverse until the landing gear has touched down, and cars cannot be put into reverse while traveling forward at faster than five miles per hour. The same principles can be applied to interactive systems. Consider these typical errors made by the users of command languages: They invoke commands that are not available, request files that do not exist, or enter data values that are not acceptable. These errors are often caused by annoying typographic errors, such as using an incorrect command abbreviation; pressing a pair of keys, rather than a desired single key; misspelling a file name; or making a minor error such as omitting, inserting, or transposing characters. Error messages range from the annoyingly brief "?" or "What?", to the vague "Unrecognized Command" or "Syntax Error," to the condemning "Bad File Name" or "Illegal Command." Some systems offer automatic command completion that allows users to type just a few letters of a meaningful command. They may request the computer to complete the command by pressing the space bar, or the computer may complete it as soon as the input is sufficient to distinguish the command from others. A more effective preventative for errors is to apply direct-manipulation strategies that emphasize selection over command-language typing.

The computer presents permissible commands, menu choices, or file names on the screen, and users select their choices with a pointing device. This approach is effective if the screen has ample space, the display rate is rapid, and the pointing device is fast and accurate.

2.7 Guidelines for Data Display

The separation between basic principles and more informal guidelines is not a sharp line. However, thoughtful designers can distinguish between psychological principles (Wickens and Hollands, 2000; Bridger, 1995) and practical guidelines that are gained from experience with a specific application. Guidelines for display of data are being developed by many organizations. A guidelines document can help by promoting consistency among multiple designers, recording practical experience, incorporating the results of empirical studies, and offering useful rules of thumb (see Chapters 3 and 11). The creation of a guidelines document engages the design community in a lively discussion of input or output formats, command sequences, terminology, and hardware devices. Inspirations for design guidelines can also be taken from graphics designers (Mullet and Sano, 1995; Lynch and Horton, 1999; Galitz, 2003).

2.7.1 Organizing the display

Smith and Mosier (1986) offer five high-level objectives for data display that remain vital:

1. *Consistency of data display.* During the design process, the terminology, abbreviations, formats, colors, capitalization, and so on should all be standardized and controlled by use of a written (or computer-managed) dictionary of these items.
2. *Efficient information assimilation by the user.* The format should be familiar to the operator and should be related to the tasks required to be performed with the data. This objective is served by rules for neat columns of data, left justification for alphanumeric data, right justification of integers, lining up of decimal points, proper spacing, use of comprehensible labels, and appropriate measurement units and numbers of decimal digits.

3. *Minimal memory load on user.* Users should not be required to remember information from one screen for use on another screen. Tasks should be arranged such that completion occurs with few actions, minimizing the chance of forgetting to perform a step. Labels and common formats should be provided for novice or intermittent users.
4. *Compatibility of data display with data entry.* The format of displayed information should be linked clearly to the format of the data entry. Where possible and appropriate, the output fields should also act as editable input fields.
5. *Flexibility for user control of data display.* Users should be able to get the information from the display in the form most convenient for the task on which they are working. For example, the order of columns and sorting of rows should be easily changeable by users.

This compact set of high-level objectives is a useful starting point, but each project needs to expand these into application-specific and hardware-dependent standards and practices. For example, these generic guidelines emerge from a report on design of control rooms for electric-power utilities (Lockheed, 1981):

- Be consistent in labeling and graphic conventions.
- Standardize abbreviations.
- Use consistent formatting in all displays (headers, footers, paging, menus, and so on).
- Present a page number on each display page, and allow actions to call up a page via entry of a page number.
- Present data only if they assist the operator.
- Present information graphically where appropriate by using widths of lines, positions of markers on scales, and other techniques that relieve the need to read and interpret alphanumeric data.
- Present digital values only when knowledge of numerical values is necessary and useful.
- Use high-resolution monitors and maintain them to provide maximum display quality.
- Design a display in monochromatic form using spacing and arrangement for organization and then judiciously add color where it will aid the operator.
- Involve users in the development of new displays and procedures.

Chapter 11 further discusses data-display issues.

2.7.2 Getting the user's attention

Since substantial information may be presented to users for the normal performance of their work, exceptional conditions or time-dependent information must be presented so as to attract attention (Wickens and Hollands, 2000). Multiple techniques exist for getting attention:

- *Intensity*. Use two levels only, with limited use of high intensity to draw attention.
- *Marking*. Underline the item, enclose it in a box, point to it with an arrow, or use an indicator such as an asterisk, bullet, dash, plus sign, or X.
- *Size*. Use up to four sizes, with larger sizes attracting more attention.
- *Choice of fonts*. Use up to three fonts.
- *Inverse video*. Use inverse coloring.
- *Blinking*. Use blinking displays (2–4 Hz) with great care and in limited areas.
- *Color*. Use up to four standard colors, with additional colors reserved for occasional use.
- *Color blinking*. Use changes in color (blinking from one color to another) with great care and in limited areas.
- *Audio*. Use soft tones for regular positive feedback and harsh sounds for rare emergency conditions.

A few words of caution are necessary. There is a danger in creating cluttered displays by overusing these techniques. Novices need simple, logically organized, and well-labeled displays that guide their actions. Expert users do not need extensive labels on fields; subtle highlighting or positional presentation is sufficient. Display formats must be tested with users for comprehensibility.

Similarly highlighted items will be perceived as being related. Color coding is especially powerful in linking related items, but this use makes it more difficult to cluster items across color codes. User control over highlighting—for example, allowing the operator in an air-traffic–control environment to assign orange to images of aircraft above 18,000 feet—may provide a useful resolution to concerns about personal preferences. Highlighting can be accomplished by increased intensity, blinking, or other methods.

Audio tones, like the clicks in keyboards or ringing sounds in telephones, can provide informative feedback about progress. Alarms for emergency conditions do alert users rapidly, but a mechanism to suppress alarms must be provided. If several types of alarms are used, testing is necessary to ensure that users can distinguish between the alarm levels. Prerecorded or synthesized voice messages are an intriguing alternative, but since they may interfere with communications between operators, they should be used cautiously.

2.8 Guidelines for Data Entry

Data-entry tasks can occupy a substantial fraction of the operator's time and can be the source of frustrating and potentially dangerous errors. Smith and Mosier (1986) offer five high-level objectives for data entry:

1. *Consistency of data-entry transactions.* Similar sequences of actions should be used under all conditions; similar delimiters, abbreviations, and so on should be used.
2. *Minimal input actions by user.* Fewer input actions mean greater operator productivity and—usually—fewer chances for error. Making a choice by a single keystroke, mouse selection, or finger press, rather than by typing in a lengthy string of characters, is potentially advantageous. Selecting from a list of choices eliminates the need for memorization, structures the decision-making task, and eliminates the possibility of typographic errors. However, if users must move their hands from a keyboard to a separate input device, the advantage is defeated, because home-row position is lost. Experienced users often prefer to type six to eight characters instead of moving to a mouse, joystick, or other selection device.

   A second aspect of this guideline is that redundant data entry should be avoided. It is annoying for users to enter the same information in two locations, since the double entry is perceived as a waste of effort and an opportunity for error. When the same information is required in two places, the system should copy the information for the user, who still has the option of overriding by retyping.
3. *Minimal memory load on users.* When doing data entry, users should not be required to remember lengthy lists of codes and complex syntactic command strings.
4. *Compatibility of data entry with data display.* The format of data-entry information should be linked closely to the format of displayed information.
5. *Flexibility for user control of data entry.* Experienced data-entry operators may prefer to enter information in a sequence that they can control. For

example, on some occasions in an air-traffic–control environment, the arrival time is the prime field in the controller's mind; on other occasions, the altitude is the prime field. However, flexibility should be used cautiously, since it goes against the consistency principle.

2.9 Balance of Automation and Human Control

The principles described in the previous sections are in harmony with the goal of simplifying the user's task—eliminating human actions when no judgment is required. Users can then avoid the annoyance of handling routine, tedious, and error-prone tasks and can concentrate on critical decisions, planning, and coping with unexpected situations (Sanders and McCormick, 1993). Computers should be used to keep track of and retrieve large volumes of data, to follow preset patterns, and to carry out complex mathematical or logical operations (Box 2.2 provides a detailed comparison of human and machine capabilities).

The degree of automation will increase over the years as procedures become more standardized, hardware reliability increases, and software verification and validation improve. With routine tasks, automation is preferred, since the potential for error may be reduced. However, I believe that there will always be a critical human role, because the real world is an *open system* (i.e., there is a nondenumerable number of unpredictable events and system failures). By contrast, computers constitute a *closed system* (there is only a denumerable number of normal and failure situations that can be accommodated in hardware and software). Human judgment is necessary for the unpredictable events in which some action must be taken to preserve safety, to avoid expensive failures, or to increase product quality (Hancock and Scallen, 1996).

For example, in air-traffic control, common actions include changes to altitude, heading, or speed. These actions are well understood and can potentially be automatable by a scheduling and route-allocation algorithm, but the controllers must be present to deal with the highly variable and unpredictable emergency situations. An automated system might deal successfully with high volumes of traffic, but what would happen if the airport manager closed two runways because of turbulent weather? The controllers would have to reroute planes quickly. Now suppose that there is only one active runway and one pilot calls in to request special clearance

Box 2.2

Relative capabilities of humans and machines. *Sources:* Compiled from Brown, 1988; Sanders and McCormick, 1993.

Humans Generally Better	**Machines Generally Better**
Sense low-level stimuli	Sense stimuli outside human's range
Detect stimuli in noisy background	Count or measure physical quantities
Recognize constant patterns in varying situations	Store quantities of coded information accurately
Sense unusual and unexpected events	Monitor prespecified events, especially infrequent ones
Remember principles and strategies	Make rapid and consistent responses to input signals
Retrieve pertinent details without *a priori* connection	Recall quantities of detailed information accurately
Draw on experience and adapt decisions to situation	Process quantitative data in prespecified ways
Select alternatives if original approach fails	Reason deductively: infer from a general principle
Reason inductively: generalize from observations	Perform repetitive preprogrammed actions reliably
Act in unanticipated emergencies and novel situations	Exert great, highly controlled physical force
Apply principles to solve varied problems	Perform several activities simultaneously
Make subjective evaluations	Maintain operations under heavy information load
Develop new solutions	Maintain performance over extended periods of time
Concentrate on important tasks when overload occurs	
Adapt physical response to changes in situation	

to land because of a failed engine, while another pilot in a second plane reports a passenger with a potential heart attack. Human judgment is necessary to decide which plane should land first, and how much costly and risky diversion of normal traffic is appropriate. Air-traffic controllers cannot just jump into the emergency; they must be intensely involved in the situation as it develops if they are to make an informed and rapid decision. In short, real-world situations are so complex that it is impossible to anticipate and program for every contingency; human judgment and values are necessary in the decision-making process.

Another example of the complexity of real-world situations in air-traffic control emerges from an incident on a plane that had a fire on board. The controller cleared other traffic from the flight path and began to guide the plane in for a landing. The smoke was so thick that the pilot had trouble reading his instruments. Then the onboard transponder burned out, so the air-traffic controller could no longer read the plane's altitude from the situation display. In spite of these multiple failures, the controller and the pilot managed to bring down the plane quickly enough to save the lives of many—but not all—of the passengers. A computer could not have been programmed to deal with this particular unexpected series of events.

A tragic outcome of excess automation occurred during a 1995 flight to Cali, Colombia. The pilots relied on the automatic pilot and failed to realize that the plane was making a wide turn to return to a location that they had already passed. When the ground-collision alarm sounded, the pilots were too disoriented to pull up in time; they crashed 200 feet below a mountain peak.

The goal of system design in many applications is to give operators sufficient information about current status and activities that, when intervention is necessary, they have the knowledge and the capacity to perform correctly, even under partial failures. Increasingly, the human role is to respond to unanticipated situations, equipment failure, improper human performance, and incomplete or erroneous data (Sheridan, 1988; Billings, 1997).

The entire system must be designed and tested, not only for normal situations, but also for as wide a range of anomalous situations as can be anticipated. An extensive set of test conditions might be included as part of the requirements document. Operators need to have enough information that they can take responsibility for their actions.

Beyond performance of productive decision-making tasks and handling of failures, the role of the human operator is to improve the design of the system. In complex systems, an opportunity always exists for improvement, so systems that lend themselves to refinement will evolve via continual incremental redesign by the operators.

The balance of automation and human control also emerges as an issue in systems for home and office automation. Some designers promote the notion of autonomous, adaptive, or anthropomorphic agents that carry out the users' intents and anticipate needs (Maes, 1995; Hayes-Roth, 1995; Cassell *et al.*, 2000). Their scenarios often show a responsive, butler-like human being to represent the agent (such as the bow-tied, helpful young man in Apple Computer's 1987 video on the *Knowledge Navigator*). Microsoft's unsuccessful BOB program in 1995 used cartoon characters to create onscreen partners; their much-criticized Clippie character was also withdrawn. Web-based characters (such as Ananova) to read you the news have also faded. On the other hand, avatars representing users, not computers, in game-playing situations have remained popular, possibly because they have a puppet-like theatrical quality that is appropriate for fantasy situations.

Many people are attracted to the idea of a powerful functionary carrying out their tasks and watching out for their needs. The wish to create an autonomous agent that knows people's likes and dislikes, makes proper inferences, responds to novel situations, and performs competently with little guidance is strong for some designers. They believe that human-human interaction is a good model for human-computer interaction, and they seek to create computer-based partners, assistants, or agents (Berners-Lee, Hendler, and Lassila, 2001). They promote their designs as intelligent and adaptive, and often they pursue anthropomorphic representations of the computer (see Section 11.3 for a review), to the point of having artificial faces talking to users. Anthropomorphic representations of computers have been unsuccessful in bank terminals, computer-assisted instruction, talking cars, and postal-service stations; however, these designers believe that they can find a way to attract users.

A variant of the agent scenario, which does not include an anthropomorphic realization, is that the computer employs a *user model* to guide an adaptive system. The system keeps track of user performance and adapts its behavior to suit the users' needs. For example, several proposals suggest that when users begin to make menu selections rapidly, indicating proficiency, advanced menu items or a command-line interface should appear. Automatic adaptations have been proposed for response time, length of messages, density of feedback, content of menus, order of menu items (see Section 7.3 for evidence against the helpfulness of this strategy), type of feedback (graphic or tabular), and content of help screens. Advocates point to video games that increase the speed or number of dangers as users progress though stages of the game. However, games are notably different from most work situations, where users have external goals and motivations to accomplish their tasks. User models have long been a subject of discussion, and recently there has finally been some effort to develop empirical evidence of their efficacy.

There are some opportunities for adaptive user models to tailor system responses, but even occasional unexpected behavior has serious negative side effects that discourage use. If adaptive systems make surprising changes, users must pause to see what has happened. Then users may become anxious, because they may not be able to predict the next change, interpret what has happened, or restore the system to the previous state. Suggestions that users could be consulted before a change is made are helpful, but such intrusions may still disrupt problem-solving processes and annoy users.

The agent metaphor is based on the design philosophy that assumes users will be attracted to "autonomous, adaptive, intelligent" systems. Designers believe that they are creating a system that is lifelike and smart; however, users may feel anxious about and unable to control these systems. Success stories for advocates of adaptive systems include a few training and help systems that have been studied extensively and refined carefully to give users appropriate feedback about the errors that they make. Generalizing from these systems has proved to be more difficult than advocates had hoped.

These difficulties have led some agent proponents to shift to distributed World Wide Web searching and collaborative filtering (see Section 15.5). There is no agent or adaptation in the interface, but the applications aggregate information from multiple sources in some (often proprietary) way. Such approaches have great entertainment and practical value in cases such as selecting movies, books, or music. Users are intrigued and amused to see what suggestions emerge from aggregated patterns of preferences or purchases (Riedl, Konstan, and Vrooman, 2002).

The philosophical alternative to agents is comprehensible systems that provide consistent interfaces, user control, and predictable behavior. Designers who emphasize a direct-manipulation style believe that users have a strong desire to be in control and to gain mastery over the system. Then, users can accept responsibility for their actions and derive feelings of accomplishment (Lanier, 1995; Shneiderman, 1995). Historical evidence suggests that users seek comprehensible and predictable systems and shy away from those that are complex or unpredictable; for example, pilots may disengage automatic piloting devices if they perceive that these systems are not performing as they expect.

Comprehensible and predictable user interfaces should mask the underlying computational complexity, in the same way that turning on an automobile is comprehensible to users but invokes complex algorithms in the engine-control computer. These algorithms may adapt to varying engine temperatures or air pressures, but the action at the user-interface level remains predictable.

A critical issue for designers is the clear placement of responsibility for failures. Agent advocates usually avoid discussing responsibility, whether for basic issues, such as violation of someone's copyright, or for more serious flaws, such as bugs that cause data destruction. Their designs rarely allow for monitoring of the agent's performance, and feedback to users about the current user model is often given little attention. However, most human operators recognize and accept their responsibility for the operation of the computer, and therefore designers of financial, medical, or military applications ensure that detailed feedback is provided.

An alternative to agents and user models may be to apply the control-panel metaphor. Users use control panels to set physical parameters, such as the speed of cursor blinking, rate of mouse tracking, or loudness of a speaker, and to establish personal preferences such as time and date formats, placement and format of menus, or color schemes (Figs. 2.4 and 2.5).

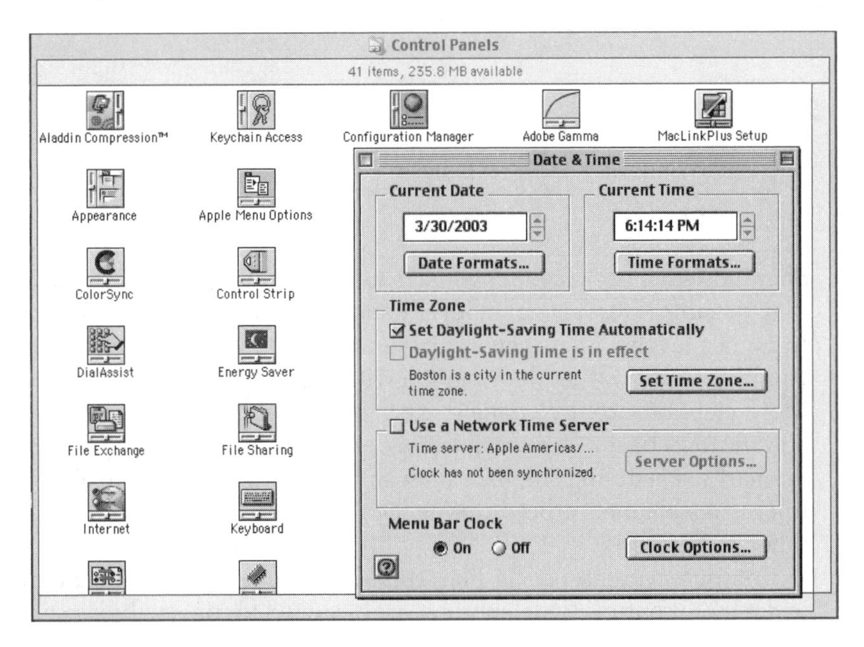

Figure 2.4

Mac OS 9.2 control panels, with Date & Time selected. Current control panels are used to set physical parameters (such as the speed of cursor blinking, rate of mouse tracking, or loudness of a speaker) and to establish personal preferences (such as time and date formats, placement and format of menus, or color schemes).

Page Proofs
Non-Finalized Files

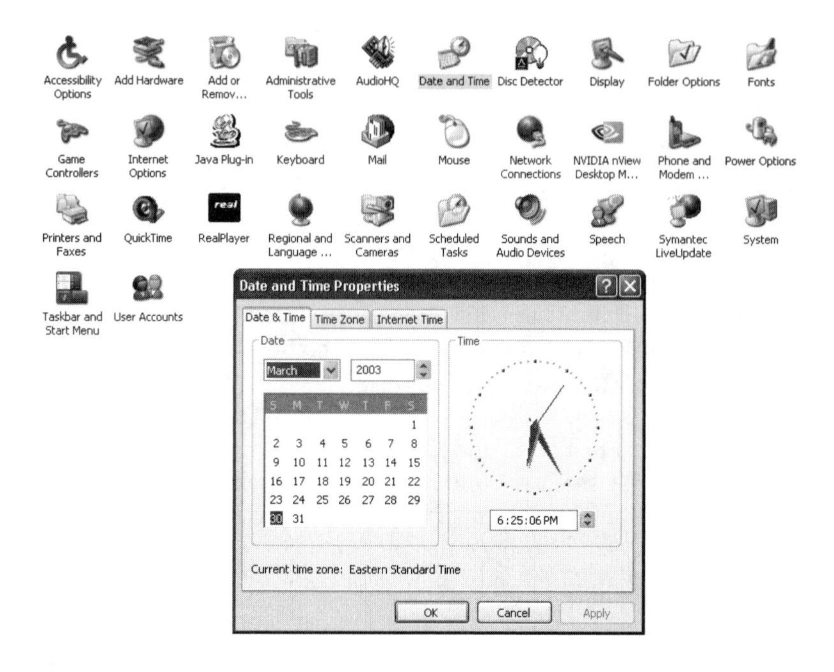

Figure 2.5

Microsoft Windows XP control panel.

Some software packages allow users to set parameters such as the speed of play in games—users start at level 1 and can then choose when to progress to higher levels; often they are content remaining experts at level 1 of a complex system rather than dealing with the uncertainties of higher levels. More elaborate control panels exist in style sheets of word processors, specification boxes of query facilities, and information-visualization tools. Similarly, scheduling software may have elaborate controls to allow users to execute planned procedures at regular intervals or when triggered by other processes.

Computer control panels, like cruise-control mechanisms in automobiles and remote controls for televisions, are designed to convey the sense of control that users seem to expect. Increasingly, complex processes are specified by direct-manipulation programming (see Chapter 6) or by graphical specifications of scheduled procedures, style sheets, and templates.

2.10 Practitioner's Summary

Designing user interfaces is a complex and highly creative process that blends intuition, experience, and careful consideration of numerous technical issues. Successful designers begin with a thorough task analysis and a careful specification of the user communities. Explicit recording of task objects and actions can lead to construction of useful metaphors for interface objects and actions that benefit novice and expert users. Extensive testing and iterative refinement are necessary parts of every development project.

Design principles and guidelines are emerging from practical experience and empirical studies. Organizations can benefit by reviewing available guidelines documents and then constructing local versions. A guidelines document records organizational policies, supports consistency, aids the application of tools for user-interface building, facilitates training of new designers, records results of practice and experimental testing, and stimulates discussion of user-interface issues.

2.11 Researcher's Agenda

The central problem for psychologists, human-computer–interaction professionals, and computer scientists is to develop adequate theories and models of human behavior with interactive systems. Traditional psychological theories must be extended and refined to accommodate the complex human learning, memory, and problem solving required in these applications. Useful goals include descriptive taxonomies, explanatory theories, and predictive models.

WORLD WIDE WEB RESOURCES

User interface tools are widely promoted on the Web by companies. Web sites include theories and information on user models. A major topic with many Web sites (including skeptical views) is agents. Debates over hot topics can be found in news groups, which are searchable from many standard services such as Lycos or Infoseek.

http://www.aw.com/DTUI

A first step might be to investigate a limited task for a single community and to develop a notation for describing task actions and objects. Then the mapping to interface actions and objects can be made. This process would lead to predictions of learning times, performance speeds, error rates, subjective satisfaction, or human retention over time, for competing designs.

Next, the range of tasks and user communities could be expanded to domains of interest, such as word processing, Web searching, or cell-phone data entry. Applied research problems are suggested by each of the hundreds of design principles or guidelines that have been proposed. Each validation of these principles and clarification of the breadth of applicability is a small but useful contribution to the emerging mosaic of human performance with interactive systems.

References

Alexander, Christopher, Ishikawa, Sara, and Silverstein, Murray, *A Pattern Language: Towns, Buildings, Construction,* Oxford University Press, New York (1977).

Bailey, Robert W., *Human Performance Engineering: Using Human Factors/Ergonomics to Achieve Computer Usability, Third Edition*, Prentice-Hall, Englewood Cliffs, NJ (1996).

Bauer, Malcolm I. and John, Bonnie E., Modeling time-constrained learning in a highly interactive task, *Proc. CHI '95 Conference: Human Factors in Computing Systems,* ACM, New York (1995), 19–26.

Berners-Lee, Tim, Hendler, James, and Lassila, Ora, Semantic web, *Scientific American* (May 2001).

Billings, Charles E., *Animation Automation: The Search for a Human-Centered Approach,* Lawrence Erlbaum Associates, Hillsdale, NJ (1997).

Bridger, R. S., *Introduction to Ergonomics,* McGraw-Hill, New York (1995).

Brown, C. Marlin, *Human-Computer Interface Design Guidelines,* Ablex, Norwood, NJ (1988).

Brown, P. and Gould, J., How people create spreadsheets, *ACM Transactions on Office Information Systems,* 5 (1987), 258–272.

Card, Stuart K., Theory-driven design research, in McMillan, Grant R., Beevis, David, Salas, Eduardo, Strub, Michael H., Sutton, Robert, and Van Breda, Leo (Editors), *Applications of Human Performance Models to System Design,* Plenum Press, New York (1989), 501–509.

Card, Stuart K., Mackinlay, Jock D., and Robertson, George G., The design space of input devices, *Proc. CHI '90 Conference: Human Factors in Computing Systems,* ACM, New York (1990), 117–124.

Card, Stuart, Moran, Thomas P., and Newell, Allen, The keystroke-level model for user performance with interactive systems, *Communications of the ACM,* 23 (1980), 396–410.

Card, Stuart, Moran, Thomas P., and Newell, Allen, *The Psychology of Human-Computer Interaction*, Lawrence Erlbaum Associates, Hillsdale, NJ (1983).

Cassell, Justine, Sullivan, Joseph, Prevost, Scott, and Churchill, Elizabeth, *Embodied Conversational Agents*, MIT Press, Cambridge, MA (2000).

Eberts, Ray E., *User Interface Design*, Prentice-Hall, Englewood Cliffs, NJ (1993).

Egan, Dennis E., Individual differences in human–computer interaction, in Helander, Martin (Editor), *Handbook of Human-Computer Interaction*, Elsevier Science Publishers, Amsterdam, The Netherlands (1988), 543–568.

Elkerton, Jay and Palmiter, Susan L., Designing help using a GOMS model: An information retrieval evaluation, *Human Factors*, 33, 2 (1991), 185–204.

Foley, James D., van Dam, Andries, Feiner, Steven K., and Hughes, John F., *Computer Graphics: Principles and Practice, Second Edition*, Addison-Wesley, Reading, MA (1990).

Franzke, Marita, Turning research into practice: Characteristics of display-based interaction, *Proc. CHI '95 Conference: Human Factors in Computing Systems*, ACM, New York (1995), 421–428.

Gaines, Brian R., The technology of interaction: Dialogue programming rules, *International Journal of Man-Machine Studies*, 14 (1981), 133–150.

Galitz, Wilbert O., *The Essential Guide to User Interface Design, Second Edition: An Introduction to GUI Design Principles and Techniques*, John Wiley & Sons, New York (2003).

Gilbert, Steven W., Information technology, intellectual property, and education, *EDUCOM Review*, 25 (1990), 14–20.

Greenbaum, Joan and Kyng, Morten, *Design at Work: Cooperative Design of Computer Systems*, Lawrence Erlbaum Associates, Hillsdale, NJ (1991).

Grudin, Jonathan, The case against user interface consistency, *Communications of the ACM*, 32, 10 (1989), 1164–1173.

Hackos, JoAnn T. and Redish, Janice C., *User and Task Analysis for Interface Design*, John Wiley & Sons, New York (1998).

Hancock, P. A. and Scallen, S. F., The future of function allocation, *Ergonomics in Design*, 4, 4 (October 1996), 24–29.

Hansen, Wilfred J., User engineering principles for interactive systems, *Proc. Fall Joint Computer Conference*, 39, AFIPS Press, Montvale, NJ (1971), 523–532.

Hayes-Roth, Barbara, An architecture for adaptive intelligent systems, *Artificial Intelligence: Special Issue on Agents and Interactivity*, 72 (1995), 329–365.

John, Bonnie and Kieras, David E., Using GOMS for user interface design and evaluation: Which technique?, *ACM Transactions on Computer-Human Interaction* 3, 4 (December 1996a), 287–319.

John, Bonnie and Kieras, David E., The GOMS family of user interface analysis techniques: Comparison and contrast, *ACM Transactions on Computer-Human Interaction* 3, 4 (December 1996b), 320–351.

Kieras, David, Towards a practical GOMS model methodology for user interface design, in Helander, Martin (Editor), *Handbook of Human-Computer Interaction,* Elsevier Science Publishers, Amsterdam, The Netherlands (1988), 135–157.

Kieras, David and Polson, Peter G., An approach to the formal analysis of user complexity, *International Journal of Man-Machine Studies,* 22 (1985), 365–394.

Lanier, Jaron, Agents of alienation, *ACM interactions,* 2, 3 (1995), 66–72

Lockheed Missiles and Space Company, *Human Factors Review of Electric Power Dispatch Control Centers, Volume 2: Detailed Survey Results,* (Prepared for) Electric Power Research Institute, Palo Alto, CA (1981).

Lynch, Patrick J. and Horton, Sarah, *Web Style Guide: Basic Design Principles for Creating Web Sites,* Yale University Press, New Haven, CT (1999).

Maes, Pattie, Artificial life meets entertainment: Lifelike autonomous agents, *Communications of the ACM,* 38, 11 (November 1995), 108–114.

McGrenere, Joanna, Baecker, Ronald M., and Booth, Kellogg S., An evaluation of a multiple interface design solution for bloated software, *Proc. ACM CHI 2002, ACM CHI Letters 4(1)* (2002), 164–170.

Mullet, Kevin and Sano, Darrell, *Designing Visual Interfaces: Communication Oriented Techniques,* Sunsoft Press, Englewood Cliffs, NJ (1995).

Nardi, Bonnie A., *Context and Consciousness: Activity Theory and Human-Computer Interaction,* MIT Press, Cambridge, MA (1997).

National Research Council, *Intellectual Property Issues in Software,* National Academy Press, Washington, DC (1991).

Norman, Donald A., Design rules based on analyses of human error, *Communications of the ACM,* 26, 4 (1983), 254–258.

Norman, Donald A., *The Psychology of Everyday Things,* Basic Books, New York (1988).

Norman, Kent L., Models of the mind and machine: Information flow and control between humans and computers, *Advances in Computers,* 32 (1991), 119–172.

Panko, Raymond R. and Halverson, Jr., Richard P., Spreadsheets on trial: A survey of research on spreadsheet risks, *Proc. Twenty-Ninth Hawaii International Conference on System Sciences* (1996).

Payne, S. J. and Green, T. R. G., Task-action grammars: A model of the mental representation of task languages, *Human-Computer Interaction,* 2 (1986), 93–133.

Payne, S. J. and Green, T. R. G., The structure of command languages: An experiment on task-action grammar, *International Journal of Man-Machine Studies,* 30 (1989), 213–234.

Polson, Peter and Lewis, Clayton, Theory-based design for easily learned interfaces, *Human-Computer Interaction,* 5 (1990), 191–220.

Redmiles, David (Editor), Special Issue on Activity Theory and the Practice of Design, *Computer Supported Cooperative Work 11,* 1–2 (2002).

Reeves, Byron and Nass, Clifford, *The Media Equation: How People Treat Computers, Television, and New Media Like Real People and Places,* Cambridge University Press, Cambridge, UK (1996).

Reisner, Phyllis, Formal grammar and design of an interactive system, *IEEE Transactions on Software Engineering,* SE–5 (1981), 229–240.

Reisner, Phyllis, What is consistency?, in Diaper *et al.* (Editors), *INTERACT '90: Human-Computer Interaction,* North-Holland, Amsterdam, The Netherlands (1990), 175–181.

Riedl, John, Konstan, Joseph, and Vrooman, Eric, *Word of Mouse: The Marketing Power of Collaborative Filtering,* Warner Books, New York (2002).

Sanders, M. S. and McCormick, Ernest J., *Human Factors in Engineering and Design, Seventh Edition,* McGraw-Hill, New York (1993).

Scaife, Michael and Rogers, Yvonne, External cognition: how do graphical representations work?, *International Journal of Human-Computer Studies, 45* (1996), 185-213.

Sears, Andrew, *Widget-Level Models of Human-Computer Interaction: Applying Simple Task Descriptions to Design and Evaluation,* Ph.D. Dissertation, Department of Computer Science, University of Maryland, College Park, MD (1992).

Sheridan, Thomas B., Task allocation and supervisory control, in Helander, M. (Editor), *Handbook of Human-Computer Interaction,* Elsevier Science Publishers, Amsterdam, The Netherlands (1988), 159–173.

Shneiderman, Ben, System message design: Guidelines and experimental results, in Badre, A. and Shneiderman, B. (Editors), *Directions in Human-Computer Interaction,* Ablex, Norwood, NJ (1982), 55–78.

Shneiderman, Ben, Direct manipulation: A step beyond programming languages, *IEEE Computer,* 16, 8 (1983), 57–69.

Shneiderman, Ben, Looking for the bright side of agents, *ACM Interactions,* 2, 1 (January 1995), 13–15.

Smith, Sid L. and Mosier, Jane N., *Guidelines for Designing User Interface Software,* Report ESD-TR–86–278, Electronic Systems Division, MITRE Corporation, Bedford, MA (1986). Available from National Technical Information Service, Springfield, VA.

Suchman, Lucy A., *Plans and Situated Actions: The Problem of Human-Machine Communication,* Cambridge University Press, Cambridge, UK (1987).

Van Duyne, Douglas K., Landay, James A., and Hong, Jason I., *The Design of Sites: Patterns, Principles, and Processes for Crafting a Customer-Centered Web Experience,* Addison-Wesley, Reading, MA (2002).

Wickens, Christopher D. and Hollands, Justin G., *Engineering Psychology and Human Performance,* Prentice-Hall, Englewood Cliffs, NJ (2000).

essay 1

ACM's Computing Professionals Face New Challenges

Technologists can make a difference on so many critical fronts.

Computing professionals can help provide insights for policymakers to enrich their options, while striving to avoid the trap of making unnecessary tradeoffs that sacrifice too many of our valued liberties.

The ACM community is in a position to take a leadership role in responding to the challenges brought by September 2001's terror attacks. Some of us have already been contacted to contribute designs for improving security at airports, verifying identity at check-in, or redesigning cockpits to give more options to pilots and ground controllers. Others will be asked to redesign systems that trace financial transactions across international borders or examine email patterns among loosely affiliated groups. These efforts win the broadest support when our decisions about how to pursue safety and security are coupled with a strong defense of civil liberties and privacy.

I hope the ACM community will show inspirational and international leadership by stepping forward in this time of international transformation. It can do more than respond to requests for help; it can initiate innovative computing-related efforts to serve the needs of citizens in developed and developing nations. ACM members have relevant expertise that could be focused to develop sociotechnical systems that prevent terrorism, cope more effectively with attacks, and eliminate the circumstances that breed support for terrorist movements. Some efforts will have immediate payoffs; others are longer-term investments in transforming infrastructures at home and abroad.

Computing professionals can help provide insights for policymakers to enrich their options, while striving to avoid the trap of making unnecessary tradeoffs that sacrifice too many of our valued liberties. We can also promote clear goal statements with measurable criteria so that we can gauge improvement and understand costs. Finally, while promoting sociotechnical solutions, we need to recognize the importance of human participation and responsibility in any system, and to be wary of unrealistic claims by technology promoters.

I propose four challenges:

1. Prevent future terrorism. Initiate internal discussion about how information and communication technologies can contribute to public safety by preventing terrorism while preserving the values of open societies. ACM should join other professional societies (for example, IEEE, AAAS, and IFIP) already discussing the pros and cons of national identification cards, refinements to existing identification methods, and other security topics. We can contribute to discussions about how improved sociotechnical systems can reduce the dangers of false positives in face recognition, biometrics, baggage checking, and biosensor networks. We can help clarify the utility of authentication (verifying registered individuals) compared with the difficulties of surveillance (broad searches based on profiles). Then we can work to determine if there are sufficient benefits to narrow-focus monitoring technologies, for example, scrutinizing selected email authors, identifying suspi-

ACM Outreach Possibilities

In response to terrorism, ACM can focus its energies internationally by:

- Establishing internal electronic discussions;
- Encouraging ACM conference organizers to directly address such issues as preventing future terrorism, strengthening communities, broadening participation, and reducing inequities;
- Developing informative Web sites on selected topics;
- Promoting research funding from corporate and government sources;
- Issuing position statements and press releases about these activities; and,
- Educating policymakers, business leaders, and the general public.

cious financial transactions, and comparing airline manifests against watch lists. Innovative solutions might avoid the tradeoffs we abhor. An even more positive outcome would be to improve transparency by increasing citizen rights to access, update, and view the usage logs of their financial, travel, or other records.

A systematic approach to terror prevention might emerge by developing process models of how terrorists act: from their recruitment, training, choice of targets, travel plans, border crossing, gaining identity cards, local preparations, and then their implementation. Interrupting this form of supply chain might be accomplished by more active early interventions and by repairing a nation's vulnerabilities. Modern information visualizations, already used by some law enforcement agencies, could be extended to support terror network activity analysis. Better tools could facilitate investigators who sift through the hundreds of thousands of citizen tips and other leads that emerge during investigations and interceptions.

Cyberterrorism is a specific threat we are most capable of dealing with. ACM should encourage increased research and raise the national priority of virus prevention software, server protection technology, and network reliability.

2. Strengthen communities. Strong communities would be more vigilant to threats, generate greater cooperation during attacks, and be more coordinated in coping with man-made or natural disasters. Since computer-mediated communications systems are a key technology, ACM can promote research conferences on open, yet safe, discourse methods. Such systems could strengthen physical communities by enlarging shared understandings and the common ground on which generalized reciprocity—the willingness to help others—flourishes.

   Firefighters and law enforcement organizations that have well-developed experience with appropriate communications technologies are more effective in times of crisis. Responders to natural disasters, such as the Red Cross, have refined strategies for using communications tools to coordinate prompt and effective action. Better systems for interagency communication systems that also respect the unique needs of each agency while giving credit and clarifying responsibility could increase cooperation.

   Communicating is difficult enough with cooperative participants, but even greater challenges involve building systems that support users with opposing viewpoints. The ability to sustain consensus building leads to agreed-upon courses of action. Technologies to facilitate rational discourse would build public trust by enabling users to verify claims, limit disruptive rumors, provide summaries for newcomers, and record decision processes and votes.

We need to understand how to build more effective online communities that are safe places for constructive discussions. Improvements might include better authentication of senders (or controlled anonymity), mechanisms to support broad participation (turn-taking, required responses), and appropriate moderation tools (to filter out flames and off-topic notes).

How can information be made more trustworthy, especially in times of crisis when rumors and misinformation may circulate rapidly? Trust is the key to public confidence and constructive cooperation. Can we measure progress as designs of these sociotechnical systems are improved? Are there best practices that can be drawn from existing systems?

3. Broaden participation. Develop design principles for universal usability to achieve broad participation in information and communication technologies. Broad participation can help encourage activity among community groups to increase their vigilance and cooperation in times of emergency. In designing systems we find that diversity promotes quality; designing for and testing with multiple user communities often results in higher-quality products for all users.

   To promote participation in the information society, ACM can do a great deal to ensure that new designs accommodate a diverse set of users (novice and expert, young and old, well educated and poorly educated, coming from different cultures and using different languages). Equally important, ACM members can expand their efforts to accommodate a wide range of technologies, including slow and fast networks, old and new computers, desktop and portable devices, and small and large screens. Further projects would expand efforts to convert Web sites from text to voice or from one language to another. A key contribution could be increased research on online help, tutorials, helpdesk services, and other methods to bridge the gap between what users know and what they need to know.

   The international dimension is important, but even within a single country there is a need to accommodate poorly educated users, poor readers, and those with low motivation. How can we foster research on the impact of technology in different cultures to understand how to design sociotechnical systems more responsive to different cultures?

There is strong evidence that open systems, such as Linux, offer alternative social mechanisms that generate a high degree of participation, pride, and protectiveness. The diversity and breadth of the Linux developer community intensifies its devotion to building better and more secure systems. Can it be true its commitment to openness in code and discussion generates greater robustness? Can we derive principles from such software development experiences that apply in larger social spaces?

4. Reduce inequities. Since terror and violence often emerge from troubling inequities, ACM should encourage appropriate infrastructure development for information and communications technologies in all countries. Many citizens are in desperate need of food, safety, or medical care. They don't need computers, but the organizations that can help them could benefit from improved technologies that operate in difficult physical and social environments. Lower-cost computer technology, such as the proposed Indian simputer (a simple low-cost, yet rugged machine for high-volume production) or Brazil's plan for building an information society, should receive strong support from ACM members. Brazil's Rodrigo Baggio has fostered a network of almost 400 community centers in which access, training, and cooperation in technology are successfully practiced.

   Software designs for developing nations would have a core set of reliable services whose instructions and help were written so they could be translated easily to multiple languages (much like what Caterpillar does for its construction equipment). Installation would be simplified and updates would guarantee backward compatibility. This would require substantial research, development, and testing, but it is a worthy and realizable goal.

   Conference reports, Web sites, and publications featuring pilot projects that refine technology for disaster relief, community centers, and health clinics would provide better understanding of best practices. Improvements to educational facilities, local news sources, and networked communities in developing nations might be the best long-term hopes for economic growth and social improvement. Lessons from these projects also apply to the developing regions of the developed nations.

   There are international development organizations already promoting technology projects and engaging computing professionals as volunteers or paid staff. The United Nations Development Program is at work on projects to which ACM members can contribute: democratic governance, poverty reduction, crisis prevention and recovery, energy and environment, and HIV/AIDS prevention/treatment. Other agencies include the UN's Information Technology Service; the UN's Food and Agricultural Organization; UNESCO's Management of Social Transformation (MOST); Volunteers in Technical Assistance (VITA); United States Agency for International Development; The Global Tech Corps (U.S. State Dept Program); Ashoka (international social entrepreneurs); and British Partnerships Online.

Initial versions of Web sites on these four challenges have already been established:

http://www.hcibib.org/preventterror

http://www.hcibib.org/communities

http://www.hcibib.org/participation

http://www.hcibib.org/development

Conclusion

The descriptions of these four challenges provide starting points for discussion and refinement. They may lead to promising technologies that would not only prevent some immediate terror threats, but also reduce the feelings of estrangement and alienation that raise sympathy for terrorism. Sociotechnical systems that respect human values, support economic development, and promote political participation can convert willingness to destroy into energy for development. Wherever poverty, civil war, and oppression limit aspirations, appropriate sociotechnical systems could be useful tools for those who strive to make their countries better.

These four initiatives could be launched immediately by electronic discussions within ACM and its varied special interest groups, which in turn may lead to panel discussions at conferences (such as SIGCHI where such discussions were on the agenda at the CHI2002 conference). Moreover, ACM press releases could describe our initiatives and identify ACM members who would speak to the press or policymakers.

ACM could focus attention on these initiatives by proposing new topics for existing conferences as well as initiating entirely new conferences. Indeed, a truly ambitious effort would be a conference on information technologies in developing nations. The USACM (http://www.acm.org/usacm) should be commended for bringing ACM's positions to the policy community, and their experience will help in presenting ACM expertise to other arenas.

To support the four initiatives, ACM should encourage more research and development on these topics from universities, corporate sources, and government agencies. ACM might offer student fellowships in these areas and honor professionals who volunteer with appropriate organizations. Since ACM is an international organization, its white papers might be directed at funding agencies such as the U.S. National Science Foundation, Asian sources, or the European Commission. Letters signed by ACM in cooperation with other professional societies would have greater influence.

Skeptics may argue these problems are not primarily issues of computing technology. This is true, but appropriate sociotechnical systems can be part of the solution. Others will point out that terrorists can also benefit from advanced technologies. This is certainly a risk, but by our visible efforts in building constructive applications, we can do our part to shift the balance toward positive outcomes. Computing technology has been used for military applications, but it is also crucial for peacekeeping efforts such as detecting underground explosions, which helped bring about the Nuclear Test Ban Treaty.

These challenges may not attract every ACM member, but for those willing to respond to them, the Association should be a source of support. New ideas often take time to be widely accepted. Our contributions to constructive solutions to these serious problems will inspire others. The ACM community will be remembered for its role in increasing security and reducing social and economic inequities. This is our time to step forward and lead the way.

BEN SHNEIDERMAN (ben@cs.umd.edu) *is a professor in the Department of Computer Science at University of Maryland, College Park, MD.*

Contributing to this article were Ben Bederson, Gilbert Cockton, Joelle Coutaz, Allison Druin, Batya Friedman, Austin Henderson, Harry Hochheiser, Neville Holmes, Jeff Johnson, Clare-Marie Karat, John Karat, David Novick, Gary Perlman, Catherine Plaisant, Jennifer Preece, Kevin Schofield, Jean Scholtz, Barbara Simons, Alistair Sutcliffe, Loren Terveen, Ben White, Alan Wexelblat, Terry Winograd, and Dennis Wixon.

essay 2

Universal Usability:

Pushing Human-Computer Interaction Research to Empower Every Citizen

"I feel...an ardent desire to see knowledge so disseminated through the mass of mankind that it may...reach even the extremes of society: beggars and kings."

—*THOMAS JEFFERSON,*
Reply to American Philosophical Society, 1808

In a fair society, all individuals would have equal opportunity to participate in, or benefit from, the use of computer resources regardless of race, sex, religion, age, disability, national origin or other such similar factors.

—*ACM CODE OF ETHICS*

1. Introduction

The goal of universal access to information and communications services is compelling. It has united hardworking Internet technology promoters, telecommunications business leaders, and government policymakers. Their positive motivations include innovative visions, corporate opportunities, and social goods, respectively, although critics see unreasonable zeal for technology, pursuit of high profit margins, and regulatory excesses or omissions.

Each sector is working hard to contribute what they see as valuable, while trying to respond to critics. Most technology infrastructure developers seek to accommodate high volumes of use reliably and rapidly, even at peak periods, while ensuring security. Most service providers strive to develop popular communications, e-commerce, healthcare, education, and other services, while ensuring profitability. Most government officials struggle to provide safety for consumers, freedom of speech, and privacy protection, while supporting voluntary regulation plans.

HCIL Technical Report No. 99-17 (July 1999); http://www.cs.umd.edu/hcil

Even if all of these professions succeed in their endeavors and the economies of scale bring low costs, computing researchers will still have much work to do. They will have to deal with the difficult question: *How can information and communications services be made usable for every citizen?* Designing for experienced frequent users is difficult enough, but designing for a broad audience of unskilled users is a far greater challenge. Scaling up from a listserv for 100 software engineers to 100,000 schoolteachers to 100,000,000 registered voters will take inspiration and perspiration.

Designers of older technologies such as postal services, telephones, and television have reached the goal of *universal usability*, but computing technology is still too hard to use for many people (Shneiderman, 1998). One survey of 6000 computer users found an average of 5.1 hours per week wasted in trying to use computers. More time is wasted in front of computers than on highways. The frustration and anxiety of users is growing, and the number of non-users is still high. Low-cost hardware, software, and networking will bring in many new users, but interface and information design improvements are necessary to achieve higher levels of access.

We can define universal usability as having more than 90% of all households as successful users of information and communications services at least once a week. A 1998 survey of U.S. households shows that 42% have computers and 26% use Internet-based email or other services (NTIA, 1999). The percentage declines in poorer and less-educated areas within the U.S. and in many countries around the world. Cost is an issue for many, but hardware limitations, the perceived difficulty, and lack of utility discourage others. If we are to meet the goal of universal usability, then we will have to directly address usability design issues.

This paper presents a research agenda based on three challenges in attaining universal usability for Web-based and other services:

- **Technology variety:** Supporting a broad range of hardware, software, and network access
- **User diversity**: Accommodating users with different skills, knowledge, age, gender, handicaps, literacy, culture, income, etc.
- **Gaps in user knowledge**: Bridging the gap between what users know and what they need to know

This list may not be complete, but it addresses important issues that need attention. Research devoted to these challenges will have a broad range of benefits for first-time, intermittent, and frequent users.

The term *universal access* is usually linked to the U.S. Communications Act of 1934 covering telephone, telegraph, and radio services. It sought to ensure "adequate facilities at reasonable charges," especially in rural areas, and prevent "discrimination on the basis of race, color, religion, national origin, or sex." The term universal access has been applied to computing services, but the greater complexity of computing services means that access is not sufficient to ensure successful usage. Therefore *universal usability* has emerged as an important issue and a topic for computing research. The complexity emerges, in part, from high degree of interactivity that is necessary for information exploration, commercial applications, and creative activities. The Internet is compelling because of its support for interpersonal communications and decentralized initiatives: entrepreneurs can open businesses, journalists can start publications, and citizens can organize political movements.

The increased pressure for universal access and usability is a happy byproduct of the growth of the Internet. Since services such as e-commerce, communication, education, healthcare, finance, and travel are expanding and users are becoming dependent on them, there is a strong push to ensure that the widest possible audience can participate. Another strong argument for universal usability comes from those who provide access to government information (such as the U.S. Library of Congress' THOMAS system to provide full texts of bills before the Congress) and the movement towards citizen services at federal, state, and local levels. These services include tax information and filing, social security benefits, passports, licensing, recreation and parks, and police and fire departments. Another circle of support includes employment agencies, training centers, mental health clinics, parent-teacher associations, public interest groups, community services, and charitable organizations. The enormous potential social good from universal usability creates a grand opportunity for the computing profession.

Critics of information technology abound, but often they focus on the creation of an information-poor minority, or worse, Internet apartheid. Although the gap in Internet usage has been declining between men and women, and between old and young, the gap is growing between rich and poor and between well and poorly educated. Less well documented is the continuing separation between cultural and racial groups, and the low rates of usage by disadvantaged users whose unemployment, homelessness, poor health, or cognitive limitations raise further barriers (Silver, 1999). Ambitious pursuit of universal access and usability will counter some of their legitimate concerns and help create more effective technologies with more effective support systems for users.

There are other criticisms of information and communications systems that should also be heard by technology promoters. These include concerns about breakdown of community social systems, alienation of individuals that leads to crime and violence, loss of privacy, expansion of bureaucracies, and inadequate attention to potential failures (such as the year 2000 problems or loss of power/data). Open public discussion of these issues by way of participatory design strategies and Social Impact Statements (Shneiderman and Rose, 1997) might reduce negative and unanticipated side effects.

Technology enthusiasts can be proud of what has been accomplished and how many successful Internet users there are, but deeper insights will come from understanding the problems of frustrated unsuccessful users, and of those who have turned away or stayed away. Each step to broaden participation and reach these forgotten users by providing useful and usable services will bring credit to our profession. A necessary first step is to formulate a research agenda.

2 • Previous Research Agendas

There is growing attention to the computing research issues related to universal access and usability. The thoughtful and focused Rand Corporation report on *Universal Access to Email* (Anderson, Bikson, Law, and Mitchell, 1995) made it clear that "better understanding of the capabilities and limitations of current user-computer interfaces is needed." Similarly, when the National Academy of Science/National Research Council convened a panel on *every-citizen interfaces*, they recommended "an aggressive research program, funded by government and private sources, that examines both the human performance side of interfaces and the interface technologies, current and potential (CSTB, 1997)."

During a well-financed but controversial study of 48 Pittsburgh area homes, 133 participants received computers, free network connections, training, and assistance with problems. Even in such optimal conditions a central limitation was the difficulties that users experienced with the services (Kraut, Scherlis, Mukhopadhyay, Manning, and Kiesler, 1996). The researchers wrote "even the easiest-to-use computers and applications pose significant barriers to the use of online services... even with help and our simplified procedure, HomeNet participants had trouble connecting to the Internet."

As attention to the issue of universal access and usability has grown, frameworks for analyzing problems have appeared. Clement and Shade (1999) suggest seven layers of analysis: carriage facilities, devices, software tools, content services, service/access provision, literacy/social facilitation, and governance. They see usability as a problem, especially for users with handicaps, and encourage consideration of the wide range of users and needs. Universal usability is sometimes tied to meeting the needs of users who are disabled or work in disabling conditions. This is an important direction for research that is likely to benefit all users. The adaptability needed for users with diverse physical, visual, auditory, or cognitive handicaps is likely to benefit users with differing preferences, tasks, hardware, etc. (Glinert and York, 1992; Newell, 1995; Laux, McNally, Paciello, and Vanderheiden, 1996). Plasticity of the interface and presentation independence of the contents both contribute to universal usability.

The 2000 ACM SIGCHI (Special Interest Group on Computer Human Interaction, http://www.acm.org/sigchi) Research Agenda focused on design of useful, usable, and universal user interfaces (Scholtz et al., 1999). SIGCHI has also promoted diversity with its outreach efforts to seniors, kids, teachers, and international groups. The ACM's SIGCAPH (Special Interest Group on Computers and the Physically Handicapped, http://www.acm.org/sigcaph) has long promoted accessibility for disabled users, and its ASSETS series of conference proceedings (http://www.acm.org/sigcaph/assets) provides useful guidance. The European conferences on User Interfaces for All (http://ui4all.ics.forth.gr) also deal with interface design strategies. The Web Accessibility Initiative (http://www.w3.org/WAI) of the World Wide Web Consortium has a guidelines document with 14 thoughtful content design items to support disabled users, North Carolina State University's Center for Universal Design lists 7 key principles (http://www.design.ncsu.edu/cud), and the University of Wisconsin's TRACE Center offers links to many resources (http://trace.wisc.edu/world).

3 • A Universal Usability Research Agenda

This research agenda focuses on three universal usability challenges to designers: technology variety, user diversity, and gaps in user knowledge. Skeptics caution that forcing designers to accommodate low-end technology, low-ability citizens, and low-skilled users will result in a lowest common denominator system that will be less useful to most users. This dark scenario, called dumbing down, is a reasonable fear, but the experience of this author supports a brighter outcome.

I believe that accommodating a broader spectrum of usage situations forces designers to consider a wider range of designs and often leads to innovations that benefit all users. For example, Web browsers, unlike word processors, reformat text to match the width of the window. This accommodates users with small displays (narrower than 640 pixels) and provides a nice benefit for users with larger displays (wider than 1024 pixels), who can view more of a Web page with less scrolling. Accommodating narrower (less than 400 pixels) or wider (more than 1200 pixels) displays presents just the kind of challenge that may push designers to develop new ideas. For example, they could consider reducing font and image sizes for small displays, moving to a multi-column format for large displays, exploring paging strategies (instead of scrolling), and developing overviews.

A second skeptics' caution, called the innovation restriction scenario, is that attempts to accommodate the low end (technology, ability, or skill) will constrain innovations for the high end. This is again a reasonable caution, but if designers are aware of this concern the dangers seem avoidable. A basic HTML Web page accommodates low-end users, and sophisticated user interfaces using Java applets or Shockwave plug-ins can be added for users with advanced hardware and software, plus fast network connections. New technologies can often be provided as an add-on or plug-in, rather than a replacement. As the new technology becomes perfected and widely accepted, it may become the new standard. Layered approaches have been successful in the past and they are compelling for accommodating a wide range of users. They are easy to implement when planned in advance, but often difficult to retrofit.

Advocates who promote accommodation of handicapped users often describe the curbcut—a scooped out piece of sidewalk to allow wheelchair users to cross streets. Adding curbcuts after the curbs have been built is expensive, but building them in advance reduces costs because less material is needed. The benefits extend to baby carriage pushers, delivery service workers, bicyclists, and travelers with roller bags. Other computer-related accommodations that benefit many users are putting the power switch in the front of computers, building adjustable keyboards, and allowing user control over audio volume, screen brightness, and monitor position.

Automobile designers have long understood the benefits of accommodating a wide range of users. They feature adjustable seats, steering wheels, mirrors, and lighting levels as standard equipment and offer optional equipment for those who need additional flexibility.

Reaching a broad audience is more than a democratic ideal; it makes good business sense. The case for *network externalities*, the concept that all users benefit from expanded participation (Shapiro and Varian, 1998; Borenstein, 1998), has been made repeatedly. Facilitating access and improving usability expands markets and increases participation of diverse users whose contributions to the community may be valuable to many. Broadening participation is not only an issue of reducing costs for new equipment. As the number of users grows, the capacity to rapidly replace a majority of equipment declines, so strategies that accommodate a wide range of equipment will become even more in demand.

With these concerns in mind, the research agenda for universal usability may provoke many innovations for all users.

3.1 Technology variety: Supporting a broad range of hardware, software, and network access The first challenge is to deal with the pace of technology change and the variety of equipment that users employ. The stabilizing forces of standard hardware, operating systems, network protocols, file formats, and user interfaces are undermined by the rapid pace of technological change. The technological innovators delight in novelty and improved features. They see competitive advantage to advanced designs, but these changes disrupt efforts to broaden audiences and markets. Since limiting progress is usually an unsatisfactory solution, an appealing strategy is to make information content, online services, entertainment, and user interfaces more malleable or adaptable.

The range of processor speeds in use probably varies by a factor of 1000 or more. Moore's Law, which states that processor speeds double every 18 months, means that after 10 years the speed of the newest processors will be 100 times faster. Designers who wish to take advantage of new technologies risk excluding users with older machines. Similar changes for RAM and hard disk space also inhibit current designers who wish to reach a wide audience. Other hardware improvements such as increased screen size and improved input devices also threaten to limit access. Research on accommodating varying processor speed, RAM, hard disk space, screen size, and input devices could help cope with this challenge.

Another hardware-related research topic is software to convert interfaces and information across media or devices. For users who wish to get Web page contents read to them over the telephone or for blind users, there are already some services (http://www.conversa.com), but improvements are needed to speed delivery and extract appropriately (Thomas, Basson, and Gardner-Bonneau, 1999). Accommodating assorted input devices by a universal bus would allow third-party developers to create specialized and innovative devices for users with handicaps or special needs (Perry, Macken, Scott, and McKinley, 1997).

Software changes are a second concern. As application programs mature and operating systems evolve users of current software may find their programs become obsolete because newer versions fail to preserve file format compatibility. Some changes are necessary to support new features, but research would be helpful to identify modular designs that promote evolution while ensuring compatibility and bi-directional file conversion. The Java movement is a step in the right direction, since it proposes to support platform independence, but its struggles indicate the difficulty of the problems.

Network access variety is a third problem. Some users will continue to use slower speed (14.4Kbps) dial-up modems while others will use 10Mbps cable modems. This 100-fold speedup requires careful planning to accommodate. Since many Web pages contain large amounts of graphics, providing user control of byte counts would be highly advantageous. Most browsers allow users to inhibit graphics, but more flexible strategies are needed. Users should be able to specify that they want reduced byte-count graphics and invoke procedures on the server to compress the image from 300K to 100K or to 30K. With additional image analysis research, servers should be able to produce a 10K image outline. An alternative is simply a 100-byte textual label, supplied by the author, already a requirement for many Web sites that accommodate blind users.

3.2 User diversity: Accommodating users with different skills, knowledge, age, gender, handicaps, literacy, culture, income, etc. A second challenge to broadening participation is the diversity of users (Kobsa and Stephanidis, 1998; Fink, Kobsa, and Nill, 1999). Since skill levels with computing vary greatly, many search engines provide a basic and advanced dialog box for query formulation. Since knowledge levels in an application domain vary greatly, some sites provide two or more versions. For example, the National Cancer Institute provides thoughtful information on many forms of cancer for patients and more detailed information for physicians. Since children differ from adults in their needs, NASA provides a K–12 (kindergarten through 12th grade) section of many of their space mission pages. Many other examples of accommodating diverse users by simply creating separate sections of a Web site can be found. Universities often segment their sites for applicants, current students, or alumni, but then provide links to shared resources of mutual interest.

Similar segmenting strategies can be employed to accommodate users with poor reading skills or users who require other natural languages. While there are some services to automatically convert Web pages to multiple languages (http://www.altavista.com, http://www.scn.org/spanish.html), the quality of human translations is much higher. Research on tools to facilitate preparation and updating of Web sites in multiple languages would be helpful. For example, if an e-commerce site maintained multiple language versions of a product catalog, then it would be useful to have a tool that facilitated simultaneous changes to a product price (possibly in different currencies), name (possibly in different character sets), or description (possibly tuned to regional variations). A more difficult problem comes in trying to accommodate users with a wide range of incomes, cultures, or religions. Imagine trying to prepare multiple music, food, or clothing catalogs that were tuned to local needs by emphasizing highly desired products and eliminating offensive items. E-commerce sites that are successful in these strategies are likely to be more widely used.

Another set of issues deals with the wide range of handicaps, or differential capabilities of users. Many systems allow partially sighted users, especially elderly users, to increase the font size or contrast in documents, but they rarely allow users to improve readability in control panels, help messages, or dialog boxes. Blind users will be more active users of information and communications services if they can receive documents by speech generation or in Braille, and provide input by voice or their customized interfaces. Physically handicapped users will eagerly use services if they can connect their customized interfaces to standard graphical user interfaces, even though they may work at a much slower pace. Cognitively impaired users with mild learning disabilities, dyslexia, poor memory, and other special needs could also be accommodated with modest design changes to improve layouts, control vocabulary, and limit short-term memory demands.

Expert and frequent users also have special needs. Enabling customization that speeds high-volume users, macros to support repeated operations, and inclusion of special-purpose devices could bring many benefits. Research on the needs of high-end users could improve interfaces for all users.

Finally, appropriate services for a broader range of users need to be developed, tested, and refined. Corporate knowledge workers are the primary audience for many contemporary software projects, so the interface and information needs of the unemployed, homemakers, disabled, or migrant workers usually get less attention. This has been an appropriate business decision until now, but as the market broadens and key societal services are provided electronically, the forgotten users must be accommodated. For example, Microsoft Word provides templates for marketing plans and corporate reports, but every-citizen interfaces might help with job applications, babysitting cooperatives, or letters to City Hall.

The growth of online support communities, medical first-aid guides, neighborhood-improvement councils, and parent-teacher associations will be accelerated as improved interface and information designs are developed. Community-oriented plans for preventing drug or alcohol abuse, domestic violence, or crime could also benefit from research on interface and information design. Such research is especially important for government Web sites, since their designers are moving towards providing basic services such as driver registration, business licenses, municipal services, tax filing, and eventually voting. Respect for the differing needs of users will do much to attract them to using advanced technologies.

3.3 Gaps in user knowledge: Bridging the gap between what users know and what they need to know A third challenge is to bridge the gap between what users know and what they need to know. A wide variety of strategies is used in practice and competing theories are promoted by researchers, but their efficacy is poorly studied.

Users approach new software tools with diverse backgrounds. Sometimes they need only a few minutes of orientation to understand the novelties and begin to use new tools successfully. Often users need more time to acquire knowledge about the objects and actions in the application domain and in the user interface. To help these users, designers need clear and validated guidance on effective tutorials for novices, lucid instructions for common tasks, constructive help for intermittent users, and compact presentations for experts. Improved designs of user interfaces should emphasize error prevention, but specific, positive tone and constructive error messages, with easy repair strategies, are also important. Other potential aids are easily reversible actions and detailed history keeping for review and consultation with peers and mentors. Systematic logging of usage and observations of users would help greatly. Research on tools to help developers provide, assess, and refine such services would be useful.

A more fundamental interface and information-design research problem is how to develop improved strategies for evolutionary learning. Proposals for appropriate layered designs, graceful progressive disclosure, and comprehensible user-controlled options need to be implemented and tested. Could users begin with an interface that contained only basic features (say five percent of the full system) and become experts at this level within a few minutes? Introductions and tutorials could be finely tuned to meet the needs of users of this narrow set of features. Then how might they explore additional features and add them as needed? Similarly, how can users understand and cope with the many exotic options in modern word processors, email handlers, and Web browsers? A good beginning has been made with concepts such as layered implementations and the minimal manual (van der Meij and Carroll, 1995), but scaling up and broader application will require further research.

Finally, the provision of online help by way of email, telephone, video conferencing, and shared screens needs further examination and design improvements. There is appealing evidence that online social mechanisms among peers such as news groups, listservs, and frequently asked question (FAQ) lists are helpful, but there is little research that distinguishes among the best and worst of these. While consumer advocates have studied the time to get responses from telephone help desks offered by software providers, there is little insight about how to make these services more effective. Best practices, validated analyses, guidelines, and theories could all be improved through extensive research.

4. Conclusion

Attaining the benefits of universal access to Web-based and other information, communications, entertainment, and government services will require a more intense commitment to lowering costs, coupled with human-computer interaction research and usability engineering. A starting point for research would be a program that addressed at least these universal usability challenges:

- **Technology variety**: Supporting a broad range of hardware, software, and network access
- **User diversity**: Accommodating users with different skills, knowledge, age, gender, handicaps, literacy, culture, income, etc.
- **Gaps in user knowledge**: Bridging the gap between what users know and what they need to know

America Online claims that "It's so easy to use. That's why we are number one." They recognize the centrality of usability, and have done well to make their services usable by many. Their success is admirable in reaching a fraction of the potential audience, but much work remains to achieve the goal of universal usability. In planning ahead to a time when vital services will be provided online and when novel social, economic, and political programs become possible because of widespread citizen participation, we should consider what research is needed to support our aspirations.

Acknowledgments

Thanks to Alfred Kobsa, Gary Marchionini, Elizabeth Murphy, Jenny Preece, Anne Rose, Andrew Sears, David Silver, Barbara Simons, John Thomas, and Bryant York for comments on early versions of this paper. Thanks also to continuing support from IBM and the U.S. Census Bureau.

References

Anderson, R.H., Bikson, Tora, Law, Sally Ann, and Mitchell, Bridger M., *Universal access to e-mail: Feasibility and societal implications,* The Rand Corporation, Santa Monica, CA. http://www.rand.org/publications/MR/MR650/.

Bergman, Eric and Johnson, Earl, Towards accessible human-computer interaction, In Nielsen, Jakob (Editor), *Advances in Human-Computer Interaction: Volume 5,* Ablex Publishing, Norwood, NJ (1995). Also at http://www.sun.com/tech/access/updt.HCI.advance.html.

Borenstein, Nathaniel, One Planet, One Net, Many Voices, *CPSR Newsletter 16,* 1 (Winter 1998) 1, 5–8.

Clement, Andrew and Shade, Leslie Regan, *The Access Rainbow: Conceptualizing universal access to the information/communications infrastructure,* University of Toronto (1999, submitted).

Computer Science and Telecommunications Board (CSTB), National Research Council, *More than Screen Deep: Toward an Every-Citizen Interface to the Nation's Information Infrastructure*, National Academy Press, Washington, DC (1997).

Fink, J., Kobsa, A., and Nill, A., Adaptable and adaptive information provision for all users, including disabled and elderly people, To appear in *New Review of Hypermedia and Multimedia* (1999). http://zeus.gmd.de/~kobsa/papers/1999-NRMH-kobsa.ps.

Glinert, E.P. and York, B.W., Computers and people with disabilities, *Communications of the ACM 35*, 5 (May 1992), 32–35.

Kobsa, Alfred and Stephanidis, Constantine, Adaptable and adaptive information access for all users, including disabled and elderly people, *Proc. 2nd Workshop on Adaptive Hypertext and Hypermedia, ACM HYPERTEXT '98* (1998), http://wwwis.win.tue.nl/ah98/Kobsa.html.

Kraut, Robert, Scherlis, William, Mukhopadhyay, Tridas, Manning, Jane, and Kiesler, Sara, The HomeNet field trial of residential Internet services, *Communications of the ACM 39*, 12 (December 1996), 55–63.

Laux, L. F., McNally, P. R., Paciello, M. G., Vanderheiden, G. C., Designing the World Wide Web for people with disabilities: A user centered design approach, *Proc. Assets '96 Conference on Assistive Technologies*, ACM, New York (1996), 94–101.

Newell, A. F. (Editor), *Extraordinary Human-Computer Interaction: Interfaces for Users with Disabilities*, Cambridge University Press, UK (1995).

National Telecommunications and Information Administration, U.S. Dept. of Commerce, Falling Through the Net: Defining the Digital Divide, Washington, DC (July 1999). http://www.ntia.doc.gov/ntiahome/digitaldivide/.

Perry, J., Macken, E., Scott, N., and McKinley, J. L., Disability, Inability and Cyberspace, in *Human Values and the Design of Technology*, Friedman, B. (Editor), CSLI Publications & Cambridge University Press (1997), 65–89.

Scholtz, Jean, *et al.*, A research agenda for high performance user interfaces: Useful, Usable, and Universal, ACM Special Interest Group on Computer Human Interaction (SIGCHI), New York (1999).

Shapiro, Carl and Varian, Hal R., *Information Rules: A Strategic Guide to the Network Economy*, Harvard Business School Press, Boston, MA (1999).

Shneiderman, B., *Designing the User Interface: Strategies for Effective Human-Computer Interaction: Third Edition*, Addison-Wesley, Reading, MA (1998).

Shneiderman, B. and Rose, A., Social Impact Statements: Engaging public participation in information technology design, in Friedman, B. (Editor), *Human Values and the Design of Computer Technology*, CSLI Publications & Cambridge University Press (1997), 117–133.

Silver, David, Margins in the wires: Looking for race, gender, and sexuality in the Blacksburg Electronic Village, in Kolko, B., Nakamura, L., and Rodman, G., *Race in Cyberspace: Politics, Identity, and Cyberspace*, Routledge, London (1999, in press).

Thomas, John C., Basson, Sara, and Gardner-Bonneau, Daryle, Universal design and assistive technology, in Gardner-Bonneau, Daryle (Editor), *Human Factors and Voice Interactive Systems*, Kluwer Academic Publishers, Boston, MA (1999).

van der Meij, Hans and Carroll, John M., Principles and heuristics in designing minimalist instruction, *Technical Communication* (Second Quarter 1995), 243–261.

BEN SHNEIDERMAN
Department of Computer Science,
Human-Computer Interaction Laboratory,
Institute for Advanced Computer Studies &
Institute for Systems Research
University of Maryland, College Park, MD 20742 USA
July 31, 1999
Position Paper for National Science Foundation & European Commission meeting on human-computer interaction research agenda, June 1–4, 1999, Toulouse, France. To be published in book form.

essay 3

Designing Trust into Online Experiences

These principles and their guidelines enhance cooperative behaviors and win user/customer loyalty by giving assurances, references, certifications from third parties, and guarantees of privacy and security.

Understanding the explicit and contract-like nature of trust between people and organizations leads to clearer guidelines for e-developers.

Ancient social traditions were designed to elicit trust during uncertain encounters. Handshaking demonstrated the absence of weapons. Clinking of glasses evolved from pouring wine back and forth to prove it was not poisoned. Now, new social traditions are needed to enhance cooperative behaviors in electronic environments supporting e-commerce, e-services, and online communities.

Since users of online systems can't savor a cup of tea with an electronic rug merchant, designers must develop strategies for facilitating e-commerce and auctions. Since users can't make eye contact and judge intonations with an online lawyer or physician, designers must create new social norms for professional services. Since users can't stroll through online communities encountering neighbors with their children, designers must facilitate the trust that enables collective action. In parallel, consumer groups must be vigorous in monitoring and reporting deceptions and disreputable business practices.

Political scientist Eric Uslaner of the University of Maryland calls trust "the chicken soup of the social sciences. It brings us all sorts of good things—from a willingness to get involved in our communities to higher rates of economic growth … to making daily life more pleasant. Yet, like chicken soup, it appears to work somewhat mysteriously" [5]. He tries to sort out the mystery by distinguishing between moral trust, or the durable optimistic view that strangers are well intentioned, and strategic trust, or the willingness of two people to participate in a specific exchange.

Trust facilitates cooperative behavior. It is a complex term that has generated dozens of doctoral dissertations, not only in sociology and political science, but now in information systems research as well. There are enough dimensions to trust and its failures to keep scholars and philosophers busy for some time, but e-commerce, e-services, and online community designers need a guide to practical action [4].

The designer's goal is to engage users quickly and establish and preserve strategic trust under challenging situations. But for many users, strategic trust is difficult to generate, shaken easily, and once shaken extremely difficult to rebuild. Strategic trust is fragile.

The extensive literature on trust offers multiple perspectives. In his politically oriented book *Trust*, Francis Fukuyama, a former U.S. State Department analyst, claims: "Trust is the expectation that arises within a community of regular, honest, and cooperative behavior, based on commonly shared norms, on the part of the members of that community" [2]. This compact definition embodies several key concepts—mostly that trust is about the future and concerned with cooperative behavior.

In shifting to electronic environments, B.J. Fogg and Hsiang Tseng of Stanford University focus on trust among individuals mediated by technology, writing that "trust indicates a positive belief about the perceived reliability of, dependability of, and confidence in a person, object, or process" [1]. To separate out the trust for a person from expectations about an object or process, I use the term "rely on" (or "depend on") for the positive expectations about an object (such as computers, networks, and software) and process (such as credit card transactions and airline e-ticket reservations).

Computer scientists have concentrated on building reliable equipment; more recently, e-commerce and e-service providers have sought to encourage customers willing to use computer networks but who may be reluctant to type in their credit card numbers.

To provide a framework for online developers, I offer this definition of trust: The positive expectation a person has for another person or an organization based on past performance and truthful guarantees. Trust is about expectations of the future. It accrues to individuals and organizations due to their previous good works and clear promises. It implies responsibility for behavior and willingness to make good for failures. It is stronger than reliance, due to the responsibility and guarantee that only people and organizations can offer. If users rely on a computer and it fails, they may get frustrated or vent their anger by smashing a keyboard, but there is no relationship of trust with a computer. If users depend on a network and it breaks, they cannot get compensation from the network. However, they can seek compensation from people or organizations they trusted to supply a correctly functioning computer or communication service. Understanding the explicit and contract-like nature of trust between people and organizations leads to clearer guidelines for developers and monitors of e-commerce, e-services, online communities, and other Web sites.

Principle 1. Invite participation by ensuring trust.

Users are more likely to participate in Web transactions and relationships if they receive strong assurances that they are engaging in a trusting relationship. They seek reliable reports about past performance and truthful statements of future guarantees. The branding process generates trust by using familiar logos and names of companies whose integrity is respected. Therefore, success is more likely if Web site developers apply the following guidelines.

Guideline 1.1. Disclose patterns of past performance. Airlines report on-time percentages for flights, and realtors advertise how many homes they've sold. Reliable periodic self-reports of performance may attract users and inspire trust in future performance, as does information about the organization and its management, employees, and history. Openness about performance and personnel may engage and assure skeptical users.

Guideline 1.2. Provide references from past and current users. Most people choose medical doctors by asking friends for references, but Web-based medical services are likely chosen by reading online comments from patients. One reason for eBay's (http://www.ebay.com) success with online auctions is its thoughtfully designed reputation manager (called Feedback Forum) enabling purchasers to record extensive comments on sellers.

Guideline 1.3. Get certifications from third parties. Lawyers, doctors, and other professionals are certified by appropriate review boards, which may soon begin certifying certain online services. Seals of approval from consumer and professional groups, including the American Medical Association and American Bar Association, help establish trust through third-party reports. Logos from TRUSTe (http://www.truste.com) and BBBOnLine (http://www.bbbonline.org) and other third-party services that review online privacy practices may also inspire consumer trust, though only if they develop adequate enforcement.

Guideline 1.4. Make it easy to locate, read, and enforce policies involving privacy and security. Although privacy policies are widespread, some are so difficult to find and incomprehensible to read that they only undermine trust. Good policies are enforceable and verifiable, so consumers can be assured that the implementation matches the promise. Expectations are rising rapidly as consumers become informed. Therefore, well-designed policy statements accompanied by reports on effective enforcement will distinguish some Web sites. When violations occur, prompt action is expected.

Principle 2. Accelerate action by clarifying responsibility.

As soon as users begin the process of investigating a product or establishing a relationship, their emerging resistance can be reduced by clarifying responsibilities and obligations. A well-designed Web site should have orderly structure with convenient navigation, meaningful descriptions of products, and comprehensible processes for transactions.

Good design can inspire trust. Simple statements of who-does-what-by-when are likely to speed cooperation. For example, a seller who wants to inspire trust might promise to ship orders within 24 hours of receipt of payment or grant a 50% discount. An auction service that includes dispute-resolution policies and provides mediation services reduces the number of its potentially unhappy users. Restaurateurs who offer free desserts when meals are late know that prompt apologies and sincere efforts to repair problems (plus compensation for failures) can win customers for life. Since shallow commitments and broken promises are dangerously explosive, diligent attention to emerging problems is vital.

Guideline 2.1. Clarify each participant's responsibilities. As with any contract or agreement, full disclosure in comprehensible and compact terms builds confidence and trust. When terms for transactions, such as price, delivery time, cost, taxes, fees, and return policies, are spelled out, users know what to expect and are not shaken by unpleasant surprises. Similarly, policies for online communities, such as how long logs are maintained, who has access to archives, and the limitations for threats or libel, generate feelings of safety and promote open discussion.

Guideline 2.2. Provide clear guarantees with compensation. Since all Web providers are relative newcomers, they must overcome resistance to change and specific fears about credit card abuse, privacy invasion, security risks, and interface failures. Guaranteed protection from credit card fraud is a necessary, though not sufficient, starting point. Compensation for delayed delivery is relatively easy to specify, but reputation records, authentication, and escrow—all parts of eBay's Safe Harbor procedures—could facilitate successful transactions.

Guideline 2.3. Support dispute resolution and mediation services. Inevitably, a product or service disappoints some users, and when the standard response fails to satisfy them, there is a problem. A crushed delivery box, a delayed medical lab report, or a breach of privacy can each make for unhappy users who are not placated with an apology or some free service. Customer service managers earn their salaries by handling unhappy users with an appropriate response, but innovative strategies are needed on the Web to avoid litigation or better still to satisfy users and win their loyalty. Organized customer services are necessary, but third-party facilitators and mediators are becoming advisable.

These principles and guidelines are merely a starting point for designers and a challenge to researchers. They need to be refined and validated in field trials and carefully controlled empirical studies in order to better understand the costs and benefits associated with different user groups.

References

Fogg, B. and Tseng, H. The elements of computer credibility. In *Proceedings of CHI '99* (Pittsburgh, May 15–20). ACM Press, New York, 1999, 80–87.

Fukuyama, F. *Trust: The Social Virtues and the Creation of Prosperity*. Free Press, New York, 1995.

Kollock, P. The production of trust in online markets. In *Advances in Group Processes, vol. 16,* E. Lawler, M. Macy, S. Thyne, and H. Walker, Eds. JAI Press, Greenwich, CT, 1999.

Preece, J. *Online Communities: Supporting Sociability and Designing Usability.* John Wiley & Sons, Inc., Chichester, UK, 2000.

Uslaner, E. The moral foundations of trust; see *http://www.bsos.umd.edu/gvpt/uslaner/research.htm.*

BEN SHNEIDERMAN (ben@cs.umd.edu) *is a professor in the Department of Computer Science, founding director of the Human-Computer Interaction Laboratory, and member of the Institutes for Advanced Computer Studies and for Systems Research at the University of Maryland in College Park.*

essay 4

A Photo History of SIGCHI:

Evolution of Design from Personal to Public

For 20 years I have been photographing personalities and events in the emerging discipline of human-computer interaction. Until now, only a few of these photos were published in newsletters or were shown to visitors who sought them out. Now this photo history is going from a personal record to a public archive. This archive should be interesting for professional members of this community who want to reminisce, as well as for historians and journalists who want to understand what happened. Students and Web surfers may also want to look at the people who created better interfaces and more satisfying user experiences.

The vibrant personality of the serious researchers, the passion of the competent practitioners, and the eagerness of energetic students shine through the photos, revealing their enthusiasm and excitement. The leadership role of the Association for Computing Machinery's (ACM) Special Interest Group on Computer Human Interaction (SIGCHI) is apparent in the number and significance of events.

Since the famed 1982 conference in Gaithersburg, MD, that helped spawn SIGCHI, the events they arranged have been central to forming this new discipline and profession. The SIGCHI leadership, conference organizers, and speakers figure prominently in these photos, but notable outsiders such as Bill Gates or Ralph Nader also appear. Heroes such as Doug Engelbart got my special attention when they attended, and key figures such as Stu Card or Don Norman often reappear. Important speakers include continuing contributors such as Judy Olson and Terry Winograd as well as those who, sadly, have died, such as Alan Newell, Ted White, and Michael Dertouzos.

Attendees at these events were often playfully suspicious of my motives, but my goals were simple: to record our emerging discipline, capture the process of communicating ideas, and remember the mature heroes as they communicated with the promising students.

It has long been my dream to digitize the SIGCHI photo archives, stored in chronologically organized paper folders, and make them available online. Fortunately, Marilyn Tremaine (former SIGCHI Chair) and the SIGCHI Executive Committee supported this vision with a grant to scan the thousands of photos during the summer of 2000. The photos were organized into directories, but we needed software to edit, annotate, caption, and search the photos.

Fortunately the PhotoFinder project at the University of Maryland Human-Computer Interaction Lab (HCIL) was well along in developing a personal photo library tool to organize, annotate, and search thousands of photos. The SIGCHI Photo Archive was somewhat different from personal photos, but the basic functions of PhotoFinder were well suited to the job [1, 2]. I spent many hours weeding out poor-quality and redundant photos, then selecting some highlights and outrageous images. We greatly appreciated Intel's generous funding to the HCIL, and additional support from IBM, Microsoft, and Ricoh, which contributed to development of the PhotoFinder software (free download and description at http://www.cs.umd.edu/hcil/photolib) and which were sympathetic to our making the kiosk and later the Web version.

Personal photo collections are distinguished by having a small number of people who reappear frequently and a chronological sequence that covers 5 to 20 family events (weddings, birthdays, holiday parties) and travel stories per year. Users seek photos of events to reminisce with the people whose photos appear and to tell stories to those who weren't there. Finding all the photos at a known event is essential, identifying everyone who was there is desirable, and highlighting the memorable photos adds value (see PhotoFinder sidebar).

PhotoFinder (http://www.cs.umd.edu/hcil/photolib)

The design goal of PhotoFinder was to allow users to manage personal photo libraries containing multiple collections of photos. This led to the Library Viewer (see Figure 1), with a representative thumbnail photo for each collection. We had a modest goal to allow users to view 10 to 100 collections, which they could arrange in chronological or reverse chronological order. Users can readjust the space allocated to the library viewer, and thumbnails will resize to fit the available space. Each collection may have a description, keywords, date, and a geographic location.

When users select a collection, the thumbnails of each photo appear in the collection viewer. Most users choose the simple grid viewer; three others are also available. Users can resize the thumbnails and choose various orderings. Clicking a thumbnail enlarges the image in the photo viewer. Dragging a set of thumbnails to the photo viewer creates a full-screen slide show.

The photo viewer has a scrolling list of names and allows users to drag and drop the names onto the photos to produce an annotation. This simple operation creates the database entries that make searches so easy. The thrill for PhotoFinder users is to be able to carry thousands of personal photos around in their laptops as they travel to family or friends. They can go back in time and find photos from a previous visit, or see photos of an individual over several years. The rapid browsing and search capabilities enable users to get what they want. Users can easily add name annotations while browsing with a friend who suddenly recalls the name of a person in the photo. This design evolved over two years with several usability and controlled studies that dealt with issues such as thumbnail sizes, annotation acceleration methods, and search strategies [1, 2]. As the design was further refined from user feedback, the need for new services grew. Printing and sending photos by e-mail were easy to add, but exporting a full Web page was more of a challenge. The StoryStarter module enables users to export the photos in a collection to a Web site. The users need only to choose titles, image sizes, and caption options, and StoryStarter produces Web pages with Next and Previous links to make a complete story. A nice example is a student's story of his winter trip to Florida (http://www.cs.umd.edu/hcil/photolib/Florida2000).

Dragging and dropping names onto the photos from a scrolling list of family members simplified annotation and made drag-and-drop search facilities a natural. This also gave us a distinctive and patentable feature that was a step ahead of good commercial packages such as ACDSee and PhotoSuite. Another important step was to add the StoryStarter feature to enable users to export a full collection including captions to the Web with just a few clicks.

Figure 1

PhotoFinder display with Library Viewer on the left, Collection Viewer with thumbnails on the upper right, and Photo Viewer on the lower right. Library Viewer shows a representative photo for each collection, with collection information such as collection name, description, date range, location, number of photos, and percentage of annotations and captions. A stack represents the approximate number of photos in each collection. The Collection Viewer shows the photo thumbnails of the search result or the selected collection. The tool tip for each thumbnail shows which collection it comes from and the date the photo was taken. Photo Viewer shows the image of the selected thumbnail with annotations, captions, and other individual photo information. The list of names, showing all the annotated people in the library, is used for search and direct annotation. Advanced search is possible by clicking Search on the right side of the PhotoFinder window.

Restructuring the PhotoFinder into the PhotoFinder Kiosk to support public access at the CHI 2001 conference pushed our team to make many innovations and improvements. We had to move from a trusting personal environment, in which users could delete or add photos, annotations, and captions, to a public environment that permits only additions or changes to annotations and captions made by the original author. We also had to strip out options in order to create a public-access kiosk that was immediately usable without training or tutorials and add networking that supported a shared database for seven machines (see PhotoFinder Kiosk sidebar). The three-day conference was a great success—hundreds of users provided thousands of annotations—loudly demonstrating their strong interest and enjoyment in finding old pictures of familiar figures or recent photos of friends and colleagues. The roars of laughter and eagerness to show photos to friends made us feel that the enormous effort was worthwhile.

PhotoFinder Kiosk

Redesigning the PhotoFinder to become the PhotoFinder Kiosk (see Figure 2) with network support and group annotation turned out to require a huge effort. We cut out many features, such as multiple viewers, advanced search, and photo importing, then added highly visible instructions and logins for those who contributed captions or annotations. After our internal usability testing we installed three machines at the December 2000 Computer Supported Collaborative Work (CSCW) conference in Philadelphia. After CSCW2000, we streamlined the user interface further and went to a help overlay design.

For CHI 2001 (Seattle, April 3–5, 2001) we showed 3,300 photos from 65 events on a network of seven machines. People were very enthusiastic, making comments like "Great! Thanks for the memories!" "This is addictive," and "The PhotoFinder rocks!" CHI pioneers and newcomers spent hours browsing and annotating, returning to bring their friends. Visitors added 1,335 name annotations plus 400 captions, and attendees brought us 1,200 new photos.

To evaluate the use of the kiosk, we used trace logs, a survey, and informal observations of users. Because of the difficulty in detecting session endings, we could not record the exact number of users. Also, the trace log, which recorded 259 sessions, does not include users who browsed but made no annotations. Thus the total number of visitors cannot be estimated effectively, but was likely three to four times that number.

We received 61 completed surveys. More than half of these respondents had attended at least five CHI conferences and were more likely to contribute annotations. Heavy users were also more likely to answer the survey.

Of the 1,335 annotations added, 677 were for the new CHI 2001 pictures and 658 were for older photos. Of the 399 captions, 268 were for older photos and 131 were for the new CHI 2001 photos. A single user contributed 163 captions, all of which were for older photos. Thus the annotation activity of users was evenly divided between old and new collections, even though most of the users were long-time attendees.

(continues)

(continued)

We received 151 requests for a total of 2,591 photos (excluding one user who requested 399 photos), and 38 miscellaneous messages. These messages were often used to notify us of spelling and other minor errors, and a few people requested that several photos they had contributed be removed because of poor technical quality.

Analysis of trace logs showed that the two CHI libraries were each selected more often than the related HCI conferences library, showing a stronger interest in the more directly relevant material. We observed that long-time conference attendees spent more time on the historical photos, while newcomers appeared to divide their time more evenly between the libraries.

Visitors would often cluster around a display, sharing reminiscences. As we expected, many long-time attendees wanted to see pictures of themselves or their colleagues earlier in their careers. They found great satisfaction in adding a new name or contributing a caption and were pleased that they could send pictures to themselves or to friends who could not attend the conference. Smiles of amusement and appreciation accompanied finding youthful pictures of friends. Some were disappointed when they didn't find any pictures of themselves. Others volunteered to contribute pictures from their personal collections, and many offered useful suggestions for improvements and keen critiques of usability problems.

Restructuring again into PhotoFinder Web to support a Web interface required yet another redesign and implementation (see PhotoFinder Web sidebar). Our tools enabled automatic creation of a starter photo Web site from a PhotoFinder library. This Web interface was designed to accommodate slower modems and smaller screens and preserve a lively browsing environment. You can try it at http://www.acm.org/sigchi/photohistory.

You can choose among the three photo libraries in this Photo History of SIGCHI:

- **CHI 1982–2000:** 28 collections of my photos from CHI conferences and SIGCHI-sponsored conferences
- **CHI 2001:** 21 collections of photos taken by conference attendees using their own or borrowed digital cameras
- **Other HCI events:** 40 collections of my photos from non-SIGCHI events, including many of the same people from SIGCHI events.

You can browse the collections, each representing an event, and view all the thumbnails for a particular event. You can browse an index of the people and then view all the photos for each person. We've added a Send Comments function to let you make suggestions and help us fix mistaken name annotations.

Figure 2

PhotoFinder was redesigned into the PhotoFinder Kiosk with network support and group annotation. Our goal for the kiosk version was to support zero-trial learning. Library Viewer was extended to support multiple libraries; it shows one of three different libraries at a time: CHI conferences, Other HCI, and CHI2001. Many hidden features have been removed, and the taskbar (bottom of the window) has been redesigned to accommodate only the essential features such as free text search, full view, slide show, send photos by e-mail, delete, annotation, help, and sign off. To protect the database from erroneous or malicious usage of the system, annotations and captions can be deleted or changed only by the original author. Only the administrator can update the database by adding a new photo collection or deleting photos from a collection.

PhotoFinder Web

PhotoFinder Web helps PhotoFinder users export their collections or an entire library to the Internet. It produces a functional Web site using existing PhotoFinder data and allows users to make their images accessible and searchable on the Web. It still seems quite magical that the photos stored away in my file cabinets are now open to the world.

Each section of the site generated by PhotoFinder Web has the same navigational links as PhotoFinder on the left side (see Figure 3). The side navigation bar allows users to go to another library or its highlights section, go to search by name, or search the names, captions, and other metadata in the database. The site also has static top and bottom navigation, which allows users to visit different sections of the site. All sections allow users to retrace their previous selections.

The PhotoFinder Web library viewer allows users to see existing collections in the library by displaying the representative image from every collection as a thumbnail. This page provides the collection title, description, and total number of photos in each collection. Clicking a collection thumbnail in the library viewer takes users to the collection viewer, which shows thumbnails of all images in the collection.

The collection viewer includes detailed information such as the description, starting and ending date, and location of the collection. Clicking any thumbnail opens the image viewer in a new browser window, which shows the image and the names of the people in the photo, a caption, date, location, and at what conference event the photo was taken.

The name browser allows viewers to look for a particular person's images in the library. This page has links for all the names in the library and the number of photos of each person in the library. Clicking a name opens the collection viewer, which generates a collection of the person's photos. Clicking a thumbnail takes the users to the image viewer, which shows a larger image and all the information associated with the photo.

Take a look at the SIGCHI Photo History and let us know what you think. Does it help give you an idea of the history of this community? How might it be better?

My hope is that preserving the early history of SIGCHI will increase appreciation of what we have accomplished and provide a human perspective on the emergence of so many novel and influential technologies.

Figure 3

PhotoFinder Web with the navigation bar on the left, the hybrid library-collection viewer on the right, and the photo viewer in a separate window. The side navigation bar allows users to choose one of three libraries, go to the index of people in the database, or perform free text searches. Once users choose a library, the right side of the window becomes the library viewer, which shows the representative image of every collection in the library as a thumbnail. Clicking a collection thumbnail changes the library viewer into the collection viewer, which shows thumbnails of all images in the collection. Clicking any thumbnail in the collection viewer shows a larger image in a separate window with the photo information.

Acknowledgments

Graduate student Hyunmo Kang has been the key developer of PhotoFinder during the past three years, and Bill Kules has worked during the past year to coordinate and manage the project. Thoughtful comments were made by many members of the University of Maryland Human-Computer Interaction Laboratory, especially Catherine Plaisant and Anne

Rose. Undergraduate and graduate student projects (whose reports are accessible from the PhotoFinder Web page) made important contributions, especially John Prebula, who programmed the StoryStarter, and Richesh Ruchir, who programmed the Java server pages for the Web version. Our colleague Ben Bederson became an active user with frequent long lists of fixes and suggestions. His experience of browsing his family photos with his two-year-old daughter led him to develop the PhotoMesa browser with terrific overviews and a zooming user interface (http://www.cs.umd.edu/hcil/photomesa).

References

Kang, H. and Shneiderman, B. Visualization methods for personal photo collections: Browsing and searching in the PhotoFinder, *Proceedings of the IEEE Conference on Multimedia and Expo* (July 2000).

Shneiderman, B. and Kang, H. Direct annotation: A drag-and-drop strategy for labeling photos, *Proceedings of the International Conference on Information Visualization 2000*, July, pp. 88–95. Available from IEEE, Los Alamitos, CA.

BEN SHNEIDERMAN, with Hyunmo Kang, Bill Kules, Catherine Plaisant, Anne Rose, and Richesh Rucheir University of Maryland, Human-Computer Interaction Lab

DESIGN COLUMN EDITORS
Kate Ehrlich
Viant 89 South St, 2nd Floor Boston MA 02111
(617) 531-3700 kehrlich@viant.com

Austin Henderson
Rivendel Consulting & Design, Inc.
P.O. Box 334 8115 La Honda Rd. (for courier services) La Honda, CA 94020 USA +1-650-747-9201
fax: +1-650-747-0467 henderson@rivcons.com www.rivcons.com